Current
CONTROVERSIES

Rap and Hip-Hop

Other Books in the Current Controversies Series

Assisted Suicide

Developing Nations

Espionage and Intelligence

Family Violence

Gays in the Military

Global Warming

Human Trafficking

Importing from China

The Iranian Green Movement

Jobs in America

Medicare

Modern-Day Piracy

Pakistan

Politics and Religion

Pollution

Vaccines

Women in Politics

Rap and Hip-Hop

Tamara Thompson, Book Editor

GREENHAVEN PRESS
A part of Gale, Cengage Learning

Detroit • New York • San Francisco • New Haven, Conn • Waterville, Maine • London

Elizabeth Des Chenes, *Director, Publishing Solutions*

© 2013 Greenhaven Press, a part of Gale, Cengage Learning

Gale and Greenhaven Press are registered trademarks used herein under license.

For more information, contact:
Greenhaven Press
27500 Drake Rd.
Farmington Hills, MI 48331-3535
Or you can visit our Internet site at gale.cengage.com

For product information and technology assistance, contact us at

Gale Customer Support, 1-800-877-4253
For permission to use material from this text or product, submit all requests online at www.cengage.com/permissions

Further permissions questions can be emailed to permissionrequest@cengage.com

Articles in Greenhaven Press anthologies are often edited for length to meet page requirements. In addition, original titles of these works are changed to clearly present the main thesis and to explicitly indicate the author's opinion. Every effort is made to ensure that Greenhaven Press accurately reflects the original intent of the authors. Every effort has been made to trace the owners of copyrighted material.

Cover image copyright © Adam Radosavljevic/Shutterstock.com.

LIBRARY OF CONGRESS CATALOGING-IN-PUBLICATION DATA

Rap and hip hop / Tamara Thompson, book editor.
    p. cm. -- (Current controversies)
    Includes bibliographical references and index.
    ISBN 978-0-7377-6243-3 (hardcover) -- ISBN 978-0-7377-6244-0 (pbk.)
    1. Rap (Music)--Social aspects--Juvenile literature. 2. Rap (Music)--History and criticism--Juvenile literature. 3. Hip-hop--Juvenile literature. I. Thompson, Tamara, editor.
    ML3918.R37R33 2013
    782.421649--dc23
                                         2012049715

Printed in the United States of America
1 2 3 4 5 6 7 17 16 15 14 13

Contents

Foreword   13

Introduction   16

Chapter 1: How Has Hip-Hop Shaped Modern Society?

Overview: Hip-Hop Has Had   22
a Global Impact

Marcyliena Morgan and Dionne Bennett

With its origins firmly in the African American community, hip-hop has evolved to become a global cultural community whose members are united by a common language and knowledge base. Hip-hoppers come from diverse backgrounds but share a set of understandings about aesthetic, social, intellectual, and political identities, and about beliefs, behaviors, and values. Hip-hop ideology influences young people throughout the world.

Hip-Hop Defines Today's Youth   32
Culture Worldwide

Dalton Higgins

Hip-hop has come a long way since its beginnings in the South Bronx in the early 1970s. What was once a local street scene created primarily by and for African American youths has grown into a global music and cultural phenomenon. The unique adaptability of the genre has allowed it to be adopted in countries from Japan to Nairobi, giving voice to disenfranchised youth worldwide.

Hip-Hop Is a Powerful Force for Global   39
Sociopolitical Change

Sujatha Fernandez

Hip-hop is the most popular music style in the world, and it has become a major player in the democracy movement in the Middle East and Africa. Political rap songs have ignited powerful protest movements and have become the soundtrack for revolution in Egypt, Tunisia, and elsewhere. Rap's ability to give voice to the oppressed and to quickly spread viewpoints around the world make it a powerful force for sociopolitical change.

American Rap Has Lost Its Political   **43**
Voice to Apathy
Mark Gunn

The origins of American rap lie in efforts to raise political and social awareness, so it is especially disappointing that today's rap is so heavily commercialized and focused on glitz, guns, and girls rather than on the serious social and economic justice issues that affect communities of color. The hip-hop generation must set aside its apathy and put the political voice back in American rap.

Rap Lyrics Are a Literary Art Form   **46**
Alexs Pate

The foundation of rap music is rhythm and rhyme, and rap/poetry is a significant mode of African American linguistic expression. Most raps are written first as poems, and to understand the true significance of rap, one must acknowledge the poetry inherent in the form. Rap is the most vibrant element in African American literature today.

Chapter 2: Is Hip-Hop a Negative Influence on Society?

Overview: The Hip-Hop Generation   **51**
J.D. Gravenor

Anyone who wants to understand youth culture must pay close attention to hip-hop. The wide range of visual and physical expressions encompassed by hip-hop—from rapping and DJing to graffiti and breakdancing—have all helped influence the look and style of what has become the dominant youth subculture today.

Yes: Hip-Hop Is a Negative Influence on Society

Rap Music Is Harmful to African   **55**
American Communities
E. Faye Williams

Every day, the African American community is bombarded with misogyny, violence, and obscenity in the form of gangsta rap. Greedy corporate executives have capitalized on the alienation of young African American men and women to fuel an entertainment industry that is destructive to African American culture. With the right of free speech comes responsibility, and the public airwaves should not be permitted to present an immoral, degrading image of an entire race of people for entertainment.

Girls Are Especially Vulnerable to Hip-Hop's Hypersexual Message   61
Beatrice Koehler-Derrick

Girls as young as five or six imitate the hypersexualized dance moves that are so common in rap and hip-hop videos, thereby internalizing the idea that so-called video vixen behavior is the right way to attract male attention. Rap needs a new generation of women to break free of the objectified female stereotypes and to model more positive behaviors for young girls.

No: Hip-Hop Is Not a Negative Influence on Society

Rap Has the Potential to Expose Social Injustice   69
Jeff Chang

Rap began as an inherently political art form, shining a spotlight on police brutality and socioeconimc inequalities in the inner cities. However, today's version of so-called gangsta rap has turned into a mainstream commercial force and moved away from its roots as a protest medium. When rap "keeps it real" instead of glamorizing thug life and going after corporate success, it functions as an essential voice for the social injustice movement.

American Rap Can Promote Political Empowerment   81
Lester Spence

President Barack Obama is living proof of the influence of hip-hop in American politics. During his election campaign, Obama gave himself an instant cool factor by making a gesture that young people recognized as coming from a popular rapper. It showed that he was in touch with the hip-hop generation, and it helped inspire young people to vote. Since his election, hip-hop has become a platform to critique Obama's performance.

Hip-Hop Gives Youths a Needed Outlet   92
for Self-Expression
Carolee Walker

Young people in urban environments need a way to deal with the serious stresses of their lives, and hip-hop is a way for them to tell their stories and express their concerns, fears, and causes for anger. The narratives in the music appeal to a broader audience of suburban youths as well because it taps into their own sense of alienation. The majority of hip-hop is positive and consciousness raising.

Chapter 3: Is Rap Music Harmful to Women?

Overview: Rap Lyrics Face Scrutiny   97
Brian Garrity

Major record labels are coming under increasing public pressure to censure offensive content in gangsta rap and hip-hop music, though it is uncertain how they will respond to the media scrutiny. While such controversy is not new to the industry, the current battle could significantly change the power dynamics in the music business. Some experts see this as an opportune time for the recording industry to ask hard questions about itself and adopt, rather than oppose, progressive values when it comes to publishing and promoting rap music.

Yes: Rap Music Is Harmful to Women

Rap Music Objectifies, Degrades, and   101
Exploits Black Women
Tracy Sharpley-Whiting

The misogyny in Thomas Jefferson's *Notes on the State of Virginia* and the fact of his longterm sexual relationship with a slave woman established a racist and sexist trend in US culture, which unfortunately continues today in rap music. Despite their significant contributions, African American women remain degraded and objectified in rap music, and rap performers and record labels make millions off doing so.

Take the Debate Over Degrading Rap Videos Off Mute   105

Michele Goodwin

The horrible images portrayed of black girls and women in rap videos could lead to violence. Male rappers portray women as hypersexual, insolent, and irresponsible. A public conversation discussing the impact of rap's degrading images of women is long overdure.

No: Not All Rap Music Is Harmful to Women

Hip-Hop Feminism Can Change the Hip-Hop Community and Society   108

Akoto Ofori-Atta

Even though they may not be as well known, there have always been female voices who have carried the banner of hip-hop feminism. In years past, that meant fighting misogyny in rap and working to get female MCs time at the mic. Today's hip-hop feminists are moving their agenda forward by incorporating a women-centric worldview in their music, so the realities of the hip-hop generation's women are given voice.

The Hip-Hop Community Works to Address Misogyny Issues   114

Davey D

Many in the hip-hop community acknowledge the serious problem of misogyny in rap music. A group of black and Latina activists has come together as the "We Are the 44% Coalition" to keep the issue of sexual violence against girls and women on the forefront of the hip-hop community's consciousness. As musicians learn more about sexual violence and hear stories from women who have been affected by it, the hope is that they will become more self-reflective and voluntarily move the industry in a more positive direction.

Chapter 4: Does Rap Music Perpetuate Violence?

Overview: The Complex Debate About
Violence and Rap

120

Tricia Rose

The controversy about violence in rap music is long-standing and complex. Proponents argue that rap exposes socioeconomic disparities and bears witness to harsh urban realities. Opponents argue that rap simply glorifies and encourages violence, and thus causes more of it. The truth of the matter is not as simple as either of these views.

Yes: Rap Music Perpetuates Violence

The Rap Music Industry Exploits
Violence for Profit

132

L. Brent Bozell III

Record companies have made millions by spreading a message that glorifies the violent and criminal thug lifestyle. The payment that rappers receive for their songs does not justify their participation in violent and degrading music. Consumers should not purchase music from record companies or rappers that promote violence for the sake of profit.

Violent Rap Lyrics Make Listeners More
Accepting of Violence

135

Karen Dill

The media plays a large role in creating culture, and it is one of the main ways that people learn how they should act, feel, and think. Therefore, it is troubling, from a psychological standpoint, that rap music is filled with so much violence. Research shows that watching violent rap videos makes people more accepting of relationship violence, increases aggressive thoughts and feelings, and amplifies adversarial sexual beliefs. Rap music in these ways directly affects social behavior and beliefs.

No: Rap Music Does Not Perpetuate Violence

Violent Rap Lyrics Do Not Affect Listener
Behavior or Attitudes

139

Jennifer Copley

There is a growing body of research that investigates whether listening to rap music causes aggressive or deviant behavior. A variety of studies have been conducted, and while the results are somewhat mixed, there is no consistent evidence that listening to rap music significantly influences behaviors or attitudes. The negative effects that some people ascribe to rap may be caused by subconscious racism.

Gangsta Rappers Can Be Effective Violence Prevention Messengers   143

Shoshana Walter

A rapper with a violent criminal past and current pending charges may seem like an unlikely candidate to teach young people about the importance of nonviolence and conflict resolution, but that is exactly the kind of role model that can be effective in reaching jaded inner-city youths. Violence-prevention programs are increasingly trying to recruit such youth mentors because of their credibility with young people.

Organizations to Contact   147

Bibliography   153

Index   159

Foreword

By definition, controversies are "discussions of questions in which opposing opinions clash" (*Webster's Twentieth Century Dictionary Unabridged*). Few would deny that controversies are a pervasive part of the human condition and exist on virtually every level of human enterprise. Controversies transpire between individuals and among groups, within nations and between nations. Controversies supply the grist necessary for progress by providing challenges and challengers to the status quo. They also create atmospheres where strife and warfare can flourish. A world without controversies would be a peaceful world; but it also would be, by and large, static and prosaic.

The Series' Purpose

The purpose of the Current Controversies series is to explore many of the social, political, and economic controversies dominating the national and international scenes today. Titles selected for inclusion in the series are highly focused and specific. For example, from the larger category of criminal justice, Current Controversies deals with specific topics such as police brutality, gun control, white collar crime, and others. The debates in Current Controversies also are presented in a useful, timeless fashion. Articles and book excerpts included in each title are selected if they contribute valuable, long-range ideas to the overall debate. And wherever possible, current information is enhanced with historical documents and other relevant materials. Thus, while individual titles are current in focus, every effort is made to ensure that they will not become quickly outdated. Books in the Current Controversies series will remain important resources for librarians, teachers, and students for many years.

In addition to keeping the titles focused and specific, great care is taken in the editorial format of each book in the series. Book introductions and chapter prefaces are offered to provide background material for readers. Chapters are organized around several key questions that are answered with diverse opinions representing all points on the political spectrum. Materials in each chapter include opinions in which authors clearly disagree as well as alternative opinions in which authors may agree on a broader issue but disagree on the possible solutions. In this way, the content of each volume in Current Controversies mirrors the mosaic of opinions encountered in society. Readers will quickly realize that there are many viable answers to these complex issues. By questioning each author's conclusions, students and casual readers can begin to develop the critical thinking skills so important to evaluating opinionated material.

Current Controversies is also ideal for controlled research. Each anthology in the series is composed of primary sources taken from a wide gamut of informational categories including periodicals, newspapers, books, US and foreign government documents, and the publications of private and public organizations. Readers will find factual support for reports, debates, and research papers covering all areas of important issues. In addition, an annotated table of contents, an index, a book and periodical bibliography, and a list of organizations to contact are included in each book to expedite further research.

Perhaps more than ever before in history, people are confronted with diverse and contradictory information. During the Persian Gulf War, for example, the public was not only treated to minute-to-minute coverage of the war, it was also inundated with critiques of the coverage and countless analyses of the factors motivating US involvement. Being able to sort through the plethora of opinions accompanying today's major issues, and to draw one's own conclusions, can be a complicated and frustrating struggle. It is the editors' hope that Current Controversies will help readers with this struggle.

Introduction

"Hip-hop continues giving voice to young Arabs and serves not just as a rallying cry but as a medium to reach a global audience."

When Tunisian rap artist El Général penned the lyrics for "Rais Lebled" ("Head of State") in 2010 to criticize President Zine El Abidine Ben Ali and to publicize the suffering of the Tunisian people, hip-hop was something most people in the Middle East still associated with the stereotypes of American gangsta rap, including guns, drugs, and bling.

But El Général's song changed all that; his politically charged rap helped spark a popular revolution that quickly spread across the Middle East, helping to build momentum to overthrow Ben Ali and longtime dictators in several other countries. As tens of thousands took to the streets to demand political, economic, and social reform, hip-hop became the unmistakable voice of the 2011 Arab Spring uprisings.

"'Rais le Bled' just strips away all the bling and the glitz of the genre and brings it right back to basics—it's just a man on a mic telling it as it is," music journalist Andy Morgan told the BBC World Service in 2011.

The same mix of rap and revolution helped two songs by Egyptian rappers Arabian Knightz ("Not Your Prisoner" and "Rebel") become the de facto anthems of the uprising in Egypt, and the protest song, "Stand Up Egyptian," by Egyptian rapper El Deeb, was sung by crowds that took over Cairo's Tahrir Square intent on the ouster of President Hosni Mubarak.

"Arab hip-hop, especially that coming out of Tunisia and Egypt, played a major role in creating the soundtrack to the so-called Arab Spring," Joshua Asen, a documentary film-maker and writer of the Hip Hop Diplomacy blog, told *USA Today* in May 2012. "They helped get thousands of young people out of Internet cafes and into the streets and kept them pumping their fists until regimes fell."

And fall they did. Over the course of a few months, rulers were deposed in Tunisia, Egypt, Libya, and Yemen; civil uprisings erupted in Syria and Bahrain; and protests broke out in Algeria, Jordan, Kuwait, Morocco, and elsewhere. Behind it all, hip-hop continues giving voice to young Arabs and serves not just as a rallying cry but as a medium to reach a global audience. Spread via YouTube, Facebook, and Twitter, revolutionary Arab rap has amplified the demands for democracy and human rights reforms and has united dissidents both within the region and internationally.

"There has been a huge demand for revolutionary music, and people are recognizing hip-hop as an important medium of expression," Libyan hip-hop artist Ibn Thabit told *USA Today*. But exercising the political power of hip-hop has not come without consequences: musicians in several countries have been imprisoned, including El Général, and others have been killed as authorities try to prevent the proliferation of music that helps turn public sentiment against their regimes.

That young people were so heavily involved in the Arab Spring uprisings and that rap was their message's medium should come as no surprise. Some 60 percent of people in the Arab world are under thirty, the same demographic of youth worldwide that has grown up on a steady diet of exported American hip-hop since the 1980s. But as groundbreaking as El Général and other Arab rappers seem to be, their music is perhaps more true to the roots of hip-hop in many ways than American rap music is in the early 2000s.

Hip-hop emerged in New York in the 1970s as an expression of urban angst, a way for inner city young people to claim their power and to voice concerns about poverty, inequality, and other issues. As rap music grew in popularity and moved beyond the country's African American urban centers in the 1980s, rappers shocked the mainstream public with their graphic lyrics and troubled its conscience with diatribes against police brutality and racial and socioeconomic inequality.

How American rap moved from politically charged content such as Grandmaster Flash's "The Message" and Public Enemy's "Fight the Power" to subsequent popular beats that eschew politics in favor of celebrating sex, money, and violence (e.g., 50 Cent's "Get Rich or Die Tryin'," Nelly's "Tip Drill," and Snoop Dogg's "Drop It Like It's Hot") is a controversy unto itself. One explanation for that journey is that as people nationwide became exposed to rap through such television programs as *Yo! MTV Raps* and increasing radio airplay, the music industry discovered that songs celebrating these themes held massive commercial appeal. Producers and rappers alike realized there was big money in making music for and marketing it to suburban white youths who had developed a voracious appetite for the gangsta mythos. Indeed, American rap has evolved into a multibillion-dollar business, and up to 70 percent of its listeners in the early 2000s are not African American.

While there are certainly American rap artists who strive to speak truth to power, few would argue that commercialization has neutralized most of mainstream American hip-hop's political radicalism and replaced it with high-grossing, adult-themed entertainment. The wild success of commercialized rap has led many in hip-hop to bemoan the state of the genre, even prompting rapper Nas to label his eighth studio album *Hip Hop Is Dead*.

As Steve Stoute writes in his book *The Tanning of America: How Hip-Hop Created a Culture That Rewrote the Rules of the New Economy*, "this is what happens to relevant cultural forces when they become so popular that they're not rooted to their origins or to the real and the true anymore—to the needs and the wants that summoned them into being in the first place."

But if commercialization and cultural appropriation can be considered the genre's weakness in the United States, the global rap scene is showing it could also prove to be its biggest strength. Young Arabs are not the only ones who have adopted hip-hop as their own; there are thriving rap scenes in countries worldwide. From Senegal to Cambodia, from El Salvador to Japan, from Russia to Haiti (where rapper Wyclef Jean ran for president), rappers are spitting rhymes for political empowerment, entertainment, or both. Hip-hop has crossed the barriers of race, culture, country, and language.

In a paper presented at the annual meeting of the National Council for Black Studies in Cincinnati in March 2011, ethnomusicologist Paige Klunk stated that American rap groups "set the foundation for a global political movement in hip-hop; it inspired Africans to rap about the socioeconomic problems in their own country."

"I think the whole 'hip-hop is American' argument is not valid anymore," Egyptian rapper Deeb told the BBC in 2011. "The world is becoming one because of globalization, there are no boundaries. I mean, right now I'm wearing jeans—does that mean I can't wear jeans just because it's American? We have to take the good things from other societies and leave the bad things."

As youth cultures around the world voice their grievances and flex their political muscle through hip-hop, fans in the United States are left trying to parse messages of empowerment from the genre that gave birth to the movement but that now itself embraces the spirit of hyperconsumerism. Whether mainstream American rap will ever reclaim the mantle of its political origins remains to be seen, but it is safe to say that its activist legacy will continue regardless.

The authors in *Current Controversies: Rap and Hip-Hop* present a wide range of viewpoints concerning the cultural and political influence of the musical genre—past, present, and future.

CHAPTER 1

How Has Hip-Hop Shaped Modern Society?

Overview: Hip-Hop Has Had a Global Impact

Marcyliena Morgan and Dionne Bennett

Marcyliena Morgan is professor of African and African American Studies at Harvard University. Dionne Bennett is an assistant professor of African American Studies at Loyola Marymount University.

It is nearly impossible to travel the world without encountering instances of hip-hop music and culture. Hip-hop is the distinctive graffiti lettering styles that have materialized on walls worldwide. It is the latest dance moves that young people perform on streets and dirt roads. It is the bass beats and styles of dress at dance clubs. It is local MCs on microphones with hands raised and moving to the beat as they "shout out to their crews." Hip-hop is everywhere!

The International Federation of the Phonographic Industry (IFPI) reported that hip-hop music represented half of the top-ten global digital songs in 2009. *Hip-hop* refers to the music, arts, media, and cultural movement and community developed by black and Latino youth in the mid-1970s on the East Coast of the United States. It is distinguished from the term *rap* in that it does not focus solely on spoken lyrics. Hip-hop initially comprised the artistic elements of (1) deejaying and turntabalism, (2) the delivery and lyricism of rapping and emceeing, (3) break dancing and other forms of hip-hop dance, (4) graffiti art and writing, and (5) a system of knowledge that unites them all. Hip-hop *knowledge* refers to the aesthetic, social, intellectual, and political identities, beliefs, behaviors, and values produced and embraced by its members, who generally think of hip-hop as an identity, a worldview, and a way of life. Thus, across the world, hip-hop "heads" (or "headz")—as members of hip-hop culture describe themselves—frequently proclaim, "I *am* hip-hop."

The hip-hop nation serves as an imagined cultural community and, just as important, it functions as a community of imagination.

Hip-Hop Nation

As hip-hop has grown in global popularity, its defiant and self-defining voices have been both multiplied and amplified as they challenge conventional concepts of identity and nationhood. Global hip-hop has emerged as a culture that encourages and integrates innovative practices of artistic expression, knowledge production, social identification, and political mobilization. In these respects, it transcends and contests conventional constructions of identity, race, nation, community, aesthetics, and knowledge. Although the term is not official, the use of "hip-hop nation" to describe the citizens of the global hip-hop cultural community is increasingly common. Moreover, it is one of the most useful frameworks for understanding the passionate and enduring investment hip-hop heads have in hip-hop culture. The hip-hop nation is an international, transnational, multiracial, multiethnic, multilingual community made up of individuals with diverse class, gender, and sexual identities. While hip-hop heads come from all age groups, hip-hop culture is primarily youth driven. Citizenship in the hip-hop nation is defined not by conventional national or racial boundaries, but by a commitment to hip-hop's multimedia *arts* culture, a culture that represents the social and political lives of its members. In this way, the hip-hop nation shares the contours of what international studies scholar Benedict Anderson calls an "imagined community," a term he uses to explain the concept of nationhood itself. Though not a conventional political community, it sometimes functions in that manner.

A Cultural Community

The hip-hop nation serves as an imagined cultural community and, just as important, it functions as a community of imagination—or an imagination community. Its artistic practices are not merely part of its culture; rather, they are the central, driving force that defines and sustains it. Moreover, hip-hop culture is based on a democratizing creative and aesthetic ethos, which historically has permitted any individual who combines authentic self-presentation with highly developed artistic skills in his or her hip-hop medium to become a legitimate hip-hop artist. Because most hip-hop artists are self-taught or taught by peers in the hip-hop community, hip-hop has empowered young people of all socioeconomic backgrounds all over the world to become artists in their own right. That is, it has supported artists whose worth is validated not by commercial success or elitist cultural criticism, but by the respect of their peers in local hip-hop communities as well as by their own sense of artistic achievement and integrity.

When revolution swept through North Africa and the Middle East, it did so to the sound of hip-hop music.

Intellectual debate by hip-hop heads about hip-hop art and culture is also a central feature; thus, regardless of their artistic ability, young people worldwide are developing into what political theorist Antonio Gramsci describes as "organic intellectuals": those who use hip-hop to develop critical thinking and analytical skills that they can apply to every aspect of their lives. The result is the emergence of local hip-hop "scenes," where young people practice the elements of hip-hop and debate, represent, and critique the cultural form and their social lives.

Soundtrack for Revolution

The significance of these scenes became apparent in the early months of 2011, a time that proved to be among the most politically significant in the recent history of hip-hop culture. When revolution swept through North Africa and the Middle East, it did so to the sound of hip-hop music. In North Africa, where young people played a central role in the national protest movements, hip-hop emerged as the music of free speech and political resistance.

It began in Tunisia. A week before the self-immolation of fruit vendor Mohamed Bouazizi became a catalyst for national protest, a twenty-one-year-old Tunisian MC released a hip-hop song that has been described by *TIME* magazine as "the rap anthem of the Mideast revolution." Hamada Ben Amor, who is known by his MC name, El Général, told *TIME* that he has been inspired by African American hip-hop artist Tupac Shakur, whose lyrics he describes as "revolutionary." By December 2010, the government had banned El Général's music from the radio and forbid him from performing or making albums. In response, the artist posted the protest rap "Rais Lebled" (which translates as "President of the Republic" or "Head of State") on YouTube. The video went viral on YouTube and Facebook and was broadcast on Al Jazeera. Tunisian youth found the song so compelling—and the government found it so threatening—that after El Général released another hip-hop song supporting the protest movement, thirty police officers arrested him. Overwhelming public protest following his arrest prompted a phone call from then-President Ben Ali; days later, he was released. Within weeks, the national protest movement led to Ben Ali's removal, and in late January 2011, El Général performed the song live, for the first time, before an audience of protesters in the nation's capital city.

Songs of Solidarity

El Général's songs became popular with young Egyptians, who had their own hip-hop soundtrack for Egypt's national revolution. Despite government warnings, Egyptian hip-hop crew Arabian Knightz released its song "Rebel" in support of the protest. Soon, hip-hop artists all over the world began to express solidarity with the Egyptian revolutionary movement by recording songs and posting them online. Master Mimz, a Moroccan-born, United Kingom-based woman MC, released "Back Down Mubarak" in support of the movement. The song includes a feminist class critique as she rhymes, "First give me a job / Then let's talk about my hijab."

The global influence of hip-hop directly relates to its popularity as a major music source among youth in the United States.

After President Mubarak resigned as a result of the protest, *Al-Masry Al-Youm*, one of Egypt's largest independent newspapers, noted on its English-language website, "Although singers affiliated with various musical styles have shown support for the Egyptian people, the style that prevailed—or at least that had the biggest impact—in this fight for freedom and liberty is rap music. East and west, north and south, rappers have emerged as the voice of the revolution."

In February 2011, inspired by the protest activities throughout North Africa and the Middle East, a group of Libyan hip-hop artists in exile compiled *Khalas Mixtape Vol. 1: North African Hip Hop Artists Unite.* (*Khalas* means "enough" in Arabic.) The album features songs by artists from Tunisia, Egypt, Libya, and Algeria.

Statistics of Success

The global influence of hip-hop directly relates to its popularity as a major music source among youth in the United States. In 1996, there were 19 million young people aged ten to fourteen years old and 18.4 million aged fifteen to nineteen living in the United States. According to a national Gallup poll of adolescents between the ages of thirteen and seventeen in 1992, hip-hop music had become the preferred music of youth (26 percent), followed closely by rock (25 percent). Moreover, the Recording Industry Association of America (RIAA) reports that from 1999 to 2008, hip-hop music was the second-most-purchased music after rock for all age groups.

There is a growing body of scholarship on hip-hop as well. Academic analyses of hip-hop culture began to appear in the 1990s. . . .

Today, this scholarship extends across most disciplines in the humanities and social sciences. . . .

The Language of the World

We consider hip-hop to be the lingua franca [a way to communicate with people of many different cultures] for popular and political youth culture around the world. In this essay, we analyze hip-hop's role as a global imprint that symbolizes unity, justice, and equality through its interpretation of black cultural and political practices and values. Our purpose is to examine the perspectives of many followers of hip-hop. These perspectives include, for example, a Japanese young person who stated: "I mean a culture like Hiphop . . . that's bringing us together like this—that's amazing! That's the power of music, I think. And not only that, the power of Hiphop. I'll say this: it is black power."

Though hip-hop is now ubiquitous, its adoption and adaptation into cultures outside of the United States have at times been problematic. Researchers have recoiled at the explicit racist parody and comic-like copies of the gangster persona that appeared in the early stages of hip-hop's global presence. . . . As hip-hop's cultural beliefs became more widely understood, global hip-hop began to take on a character of its own, reflecting the culture, creativity, and local styles of the youth who embraced and produced it. Hip-hop is now a multibillion-dollar global industry that continues to grow and diversify, but its impact remains underreported; often overlooked is the fact that hip-hop influences not only conventional "rap music," but also all forms of popular music as well as radio, music, television, film, advertising, and digital media throughout the world.

The Internet has added a new and transformative dimension to local and global hip-hop cultures and communities.

Local and Global

Though commercial hip-hop represents a significant part of the music industry, it is only a fraction of the artistic production and performance of hip-hop culture, most of which is local. Every populated continent (and most countries) have thousands of local hip-hop scenes shaped by artistic and cultural practices that are produced, defined, and sustained primarily by youth in their own neighborhoods and communities. In the United States, these scenes are generally described as *underground hip-hop*, both to characterize their critical challenge to conventional norms and to distinguish them from commercial hip-hop. And as it turns out, the underground is more densely populated and deeply substantive than the commercial cultural space on hip-hop's surface. The Internet has added a new and transformative dimension to local and global hip-hop cultures and communities, empowering young people to document and distribute their personal and local art, ideas, and experiences. These local scenes are rarely financed by multinational media corporations yet are more essential to hip-hop culture and the hip-hop nation than commercial production. Commercial production could end, but hip-hop culture would continue, and even thrive, through local scenes.

Some observers have conceived of the movement of hip-hop culture around the globe as a hip-hop diaspora that shares characteristics of ethnic constructions of diaspora. Global hip-hop scenes are sometimes (quite accurately) described as *translocal* because they so often represent complex cultural, artistic, and political dialogues between local innovations of diverse hip-hop art forms; transcultural interactions between local hip-hop scenes in cities and nations outside of the United States; and exchanges between local scenes and U.S.-based hip-hop media.

While multiethnic collaboration produced early hip-hop forms, African Americans played a vital cultural and political role in its development.

While the translocal dynamics of the hip-hop diaspora foster countless routes of cultural interaction and exchange, at least two major routes of cultural globalization are at the crossroads of these numerous pathways. African American culture and African diasporic cultural forms are integral to the formation of both these major routes. Here, we focus primarily on hip-hop music, but the routes characterize other hip-hop art forms as well.

Tracing Origins

The first route of diaspora relates to the origins of hip-hop culture. While hip-hop may have emerged in New York in the 1970s, many of its diverse global and multicultural beginnings can be tied to African diasporic cultural forms and communities. Especially in the case of rapping/rhyming, it is almost im-

possible to isolate a single cultural trajectory because the aesthetic and linguistic features of lyrical rhyming can be found
throughout Africa and the Caribbean as well as the United
States. Many of the young black and Latino artists who col-
laborated in the development of hip-hop culture in New York
were recent immigrants from the Caribbean and, therefore,
were shaped by a range of African diasporic cultures. . . .

African American Influence

The second major route of hip-hop culture is its movement
into local youth cultures around the world. Soon after it was
developed in the United States, hip-hop culture traveled as
part of the larger processes of America's global media distribution. While multiethnic collaboration produced early hip-
hop forms, African Americans played a vital cultural and political role in its development. As African American studies
scholar Imani Perry argues, "[P]romiscuous composition does
not destroy cultural identity. . . . The African aesthetic origins
of hip hop, as with all black American music, allows for it to
have a shared resonance among a wide range of diasporic and
continental Africans." Moreover, in addition to representing a
shared cultural terrain for members of international African
diasporic cultures, these African aesthetics have also shaped
the aesthetic consciousness and tastes of non-African Americans for centuries. The world's youth have responded with a
stunning proliferation of hip-hop-based artistic and cultural
production.

Aside from being translocal, the movement of hip-hop between local and global contexts can also be explained by the
concept of *glocalization*: that is, simultaneously engaging the
intersections of global and local dynamics. . . .

Consequently, global hip-hop cultures retain many quali-
tative features of African diasporic and U.S.-based hip-hop

cultures while simultaneously engaging in dynamic and prolific processes of aesthetic innovation, production, and diversification.

Along with hip-hop's cultural norm of inclusion, global hip-hop remains symbolically associated with African Americans. It has incorporated many aspects of African American language ideology, even when the English language itself is not part of a particular expression of hip-hop culture. In other words,

> it is not mere words and expressions that create a bond among hiphop followers throughout the world. Rather, it is based on African American language ideology where the words signify multiple meanings and critiques of power. Hiphop presents African American English (AAE) as a symbolic and politicized dialect where speakers are aware of complex and contradictory processes of stigmatization, valorization and social control. The hip-hop speech community is not necessarily linguistically and physically located but rather bound by this shared language ideology as part of politics, culture, social conditions, and norms, values, and attitude.

Hip-hop language ideology remains central to the construction and continuation of all hip-hop cultures, local and global. The use of dialects and national languages, including complex code-switching practices, serves as a declaration that hip-hop culture enables all citizens of the hip-hop nation to reclaim and create a range of contested languages, identities, and powers.

Hip-Hop Defines Today's Youth Culture Worldwide

Dalton Higgins

Dalton Higgins is a multimedia pop culture critic whose work has been published in prominent urban culture magazines, including Source, Vibe, *and* Urb. *He is the author of* Hip Hop World: A Groundwork Guide *and coauthor of the book* Hip Hop, *as well as a music programmer at Canada's Centre of Contemporary Culture in Toronto.*

It's a hip hop world, and you're just living in it. For most music-addicted earthlings, hip hop culture is the predominant global youth subculture of today. For the non-music initiated, hip hop has become the black, jewelry-laden elephant in a room filled with rock, country and classical music—an attention-grabber whose influence is impossible to miss on the daily news, in school playgrounds, during water cooler conversations or in a political debate.

What is hip hop, and why should you care about it? Hip hop—a term coined by pioneering rapper Space Cowboy in the early 1970s to mimic a scat and then popularized later by rapper Lovebug Starski—is quite simply the world's leading counterculture, subculture and youth culture. Hip hop encompasses tour distinct elements: deejaying (the manipulation of pre-recorded music), breakdancing (dance), rapping/emceeing (vocalizing) and graffiti (visual art).

Commercial Success

For starters, curious onlookers have to acknowledge its success as a massive chart-topping, revenue-generating music movement. When rapper Jay-Z's (Shawn Carter) *American Gangster* disc opened on top of the pop charts in 2007, that gave him ten *Billboard* number one albums in ten years, tying him with the King of Rock, Elvis Presley, for the most chart-toppers by a solo artist. Likewise, at a time when CD sales are plummeting, rapper Lil Wayne's *Tha Carter III* was the number one selling album of 2008 in the US, scanning an astounding three million units.

Forty-plus years after its birth, hip hop has officially grown up and left the hood.

Much has been written about hip hop's gritty African American origins in the South Bronx, but the primary American consumers are young suburban whites whose fascination with black youth culture has led to Caucasian rappers Eminem and the Beastie Boys becoming creators of both the fastest selling rap album in history (*The Marshall Mathers LP*) and the first rap album to go number one on the *Billboard* album charts (*Licensed to Ill*), respectively. Once a predominantly African American youth form of expression, or as legendary hip hop group Public Enemy's lead vocalist Chuck D once called it, the "black people's CNN," rap has taken root around the world as a primary news source for disenfranchised Asian, South Asian, First Nations, Latin American, Australasian, African, Middle Eastern and European publics.

Forty-plus years after its birth, hip hop has officially grown up and left the hood. Hip hoppers own palatial estates in exclusive gated communities and are world travelers racking up Air Miles in abundance.

From New York to Nigeria, hip hop is so wildly popular that it's crossing continents and oceans, and by many accounts its brightest future star might come in the form of an already wealthy, bi-racial (Jewish/black), Lil Wayne-tutored Canadian rapper named Drake. The incorporation, appropriation and wholesale celebration of the music has taken shape internationally, far from its American birthplace. Take Japan, where despite language barriers many Japanese youth have aped African American rappers' stylings by tanning their skin dark brown (*ganguro* or "blackface") and wearing cornrows and dreadlocks. In Cuba, former president Fidel Castro refers to rap music as the "vanguard of the Revolution." In Iran, heads of state complain that rap's obscene lyrics diminish Islamic values, and its influence is so pervasive that it has been officially banned. In France, it's considered the unofficial voice of the *banlieues*—the impoverished suburbs where African and Arab youth have staged violent anti-racism riots. Native American and aboriginal Canadian youth work out of the tradition or spoken-word iconoclast John Trudell, rapping out against past and present wrongdoings in their respective reserves and communities.

During the 1980s, Reaganomics wiped out inner-city school music funding programs in the US, leaving low-income youth to their own devices.

A Multicultural Movement

In North America, no comparable art form or music genre draws so many multiculti consumers to cash registers, music downloading websites and live concerts. Cultural critics point out that at rock'n'roll, classical or country music concerts, sometimes the only things that are "of color" are the stage curtains—and even them curtains ain't got no soul. Rap music, on the other hand, is anti-classical, a UN-friendly music with dozens upon dozens of subgenres to accommodate and account for the full range of experiences that make up the human condition—irrespective of one's race, gender, age or geography.

If you're gay or lesbian, there's a burgeoning Homo Hop movement. If you like your violence and sex gratuitous, there are large Gangsta Rap and Horrorcore Rap factions. If you're Jewish or a born-again Christian, the Klezmer or Christian Rap scenes might suit your fancy. And if you're a geek and rap music seems altogether too hipster and cool to comprehend, there's a large Nerdcore Rap movement where you and fellow squares can sink your cerebellums into raps about deoxyribonucleic acid patterns and nuclear physics.

Hip hop's adaptability becomes even more marked internationally because at its genesis rap music essentially involves creating something out of nothing. During the 1980s, Reaganomics wiped out inner-city school music funding programs in the US, leaving low-income youth to their own devices. Manipulating vinyl records on turntables to make music replaced violin and horn sections, and spoken-word diatribes replaced organized vocal choir practices. Today, in a similar vein, Native American youth on reserves don't need to be classically trained in a musical instrument or attend a costly music conservatory to create rap music. And neither do youth in Africa, the poorest continent in the world, where the rap scene is blossoming at a faster pace than in any other region. Groups can simply utilize their lips, tongues and mouths to create the vocal percussion music—or "human beat box" sounds usually created by drum machine-produced beats— that forms the backbone of some of the best universal rap tracks of all time, like "La Di Da Di" by Doug E. Fresh.

An Unrepentant Outlaw

But don't get it twisted. The world is not a greater place because of rap music. The genre is not a panacea for global famine, nor is it encouraging us to hold hands and sing "Kumbaya" with our multicultured brothers and sisters around the planet. Not even close. Rap music actually dominates headlines for being quite the opposite—an unrepentant outlaw music that magnifies the darker side of black.

Despite societal well-wishers hoping to see some sort of Obamaian racial progress shift taking place under the aegis of hip hop, when we look at real measurements of equality— access to education, housing, politics—we can see that it's just not happening fast enough. Sure, youth from around the world from all cultural backgrounds are downloading the same Young Jeezy songs as a collective global unit and fanbase. But the economic conditions between them aren't changing much. What exactly are privileged Western rap audiences—who are listening to the same rap music as say youth in Brazilian favelas—doing to eradicate extreme poverty in Rio? Isn't that what rap was intended to do—speak and act out against oppression—not just rhyme and dance to it?

Rappers speak about the beauty and ugliness of the world with equal candor, putting up a sharp mirror to reality.

This is the crafty nature of rap. It acts as a virtual magnet for controversy and scandal because rap music's vanguards spend much of their recording time replaying what the real issues are, including what dystopia looks, smells and feels like, with their words. It's a pure artistic response to oppression— protest music where art truly imitates life, its music intended to play back society's most celebratory and inflammatory aspects.

Raw and Uncut

As politicians increasingly refuse to address genuine social inequalities, rappers speak about the beauty and ugliness of the world with equal candor, putting up a sharp mirror to reality. And they've received heavy verbal critiques for coming off so raw and uncut. Some of the genre's most cogent songs, for example, come in the form of blunt responses to police brutality in African American communities. They include anthems like "F--- Tha Police," a searing indictment of racial profiling by the LAPD (Los Angeles Police Department) recorded by one of rap's most influential groups, N.W.A. (Niggaz With Attitude), and musically re-tooled by one of its greatest producers, the late J Dilla, to address Detroit area police all the way to Ice-T's "Cop Killer," which calls for frustrated victims of anti-black police misconduct to "dust some cops off" (shoot or stab crooked cops). Clearly, the rapperati have no intention of getting Rodney Kinged, and aren't afraid to tell you.

When the music is not taking vicious verbal swipes at injustices, it's doling out bushels of lyrics that carry some of the most offensive words in the English language. A mini-alphabet of forbidden words, including the B- and F word, appear with nauseating frequency. These are words that don't get remote consideration for inclusion on the CDs of other music genres. And would the use of the explosive N-word be debated today on CNN, in barbershops or in strip malls around the world if not for hip hop? Rap is the only genre of music where the term is widely used, despite most of its leading figures being African American, the community for whom the word was created by racists to disparage. N-word debates have flared up frequently in the US over the last few years, from shock jocks Don Imus to Bounty Hunter Duane "Dog" Chapman to *Seinfeld*'s Michael "Kramer" Richards—all non-black performers who've used the form, implicitly claiming they are taking the lead from hip hop. Critics have also long argued that rap music's sexually explicit lyrics—where the use of "bitch" and "ho" to describe women and the unrepentant use of the word "fag(got)" are commonplace—contribute to the moral breakdown of society.

Who Profits?

Who's to blame for all of this? Who really profits from the cartoonish rap stereotypes of young black maledom that African Americans have been trying to shake for decades? Some argue that hip hop is simply a byproduct of a society that is equally foul-mouthed, sexist, racist and homophobic. Should the African American community be held accountable for the dissemination of such vile, lewd language and imagery? Or does the responsibility lie with the largely non-black recording label presidents of multimillion-dollar corporations who draft up and sign contracts with these musicians? Is there a reason many non-Western hip hop artists and critics have held their tongues in debates over the use of the N-word? Are black community broadcasters like BET (Black Entertainment Television) that traffic the negative elements of the culture to global audiences complicit? When BET rotates graphically sexist videos to audiences in Canada and the UK around the clock, are they aware of the global effects on their young female—and male—constituencies?

Hip-Hop's Potential

Once a form of social protest in the United States, rap appears to be anything but that now. Outside of the US, where rap music is articulating and addressing local political and social concerns, it presents a remarkable contrast. Tapping into hip hop's potential as a force for social change should be easy to realize, given that it boasts an active, captive, global youth base. But can we realistically expect solutions to complex world problems from teens and twenty-something rappers? More importantly, is hip hop immune from the same historical processes that turned historically black musics like jazz and rock'n'roll into pale shades of their former selves, genres enjoyed, profited from and largely consisting of performers from every other ethnic group but that of the creators?

As for the future of rap, are performers still able to sing the blues, or authentically rap about the 'hood, when some of the conditions that created rap have changed? Or since its vanguards such as so-called "gangsta" rappers Ice Cube and Snoop Dogg have become multimillionaires?

Hip-Hop Is a Powerful Force for Global Sociopolitical Change

Sujatha Fernandez

Sujatha Fernandez is an associate professor of sociology at Queens College and the Graduate Center, City University of New York, and the author of Close to the Edge: In Search of the Global Hip Hop Generation.

Def Jam will probably never sign them, but Cheikh Oumar Cyrille Touré, from a small town about 100 miles southeast of Dakar, Senegal, and Hamada Ben Amor, a 22-year-old man from a port city 170 miles southeast of Tunis, may be two of the most influential rappers in the history of hip-hop.

Mr. Touré, aka Thiat ("Junior"), and Mr. Ben Amor, aka El Général, both wrote protest songs that led to their arrests and generated powerful political movements. "We are drowning in hunger and unemployment," spits Thiat on "Coup 2 Gueule" (from a phrase meaning "rant") with the Keurgui Crew. El Général's song "Head of State" addresses the now-deposed [Tunisian] President Zine el-Abidine Ben Ali over a plaintive background beat. "A lot of money was pledged for projects and infrastructure/Schools, hospitals, buildings, houses/but the sons of dogs swallowed it in their big bellies." Later, he rhymes, "I know people have a lot to say in their hearts, but no way to convey it." The song acted as sluice gates for the release of anger that until then was being expressed clandestinely, if at all.

The Language of the World

During the recent wave of revolutions across the Arab world and the protests against illegitimate presidents in African countries like Guinea and Djibouti, rap music has played a

Sujatha Fernandez, "The Mixtape of the Revolution," *New York Times*, January 29, 2012.

critical role in articulating citizen discontent over poverty, rising food prices, blackouts, unemployment, police repression and political corruption. Rap songs in Arabic in particular—the new lingua franca [a language used as a bridge between people who do not speak the same native tongue] of the hip-hop world—have spread through YouTube, Facebook, mixtapes, ringtones and MP3s from Tunisia to Egypt, Libya and Algeria, helping to disseminate ideas and anthems as the insurrections progressed. El Général, for example, was featured on a mixtape put out by the dissident group Khalas (Enough) in Libya, which also included songs like "Tripoli Is Calling" and "Dirty Colonel."

Rappers report in a direct manner that cuts through political subterfuge.

Why has rap—an American music that in its early global spread was associated with thuggery and violence—come to be so highly influential in these regions? After all, rappers are not the only musicians involved in politics. Late last week [January 2012], protests erupted when Youssou N'Dour, a Senegalese singer of mbalax, a fusion of traditional music with Latin, pop and jazz, was barred by a constitutional court from pursuing a run for president. But mbalax singers are typically seen as older entertainers who often support the government in power. In contrast, rappers, according to the Senegalese rapper Keyti, "are closer to the streets and can bring into their music the general feeling of frustration among people."

Rap Cuts to the Heart of the Matter

Another reason is the oratorical style rap employs: rappers report in a direct manner that cuts through political subterfuge. Rapping can simulate a political speech or address, rhetorical conventions that are generally inaccessible to the marginal youth who form the base of this movement. And in places like Senegal, rap follows in the oral traditions of West African griots, who often used rhyming verse to evaluate their political leaders. "M.C.'s are the modern griot," Papa Moussa Lo, aka Waterflow, told me in an interview a few weeks ago. "They are taking over the role of representing the people."

Although many of these rappers style themselves as revolutionary upstarts, they are most concerned with protecting a constitutional order that they see as being trampled by unscrupulous politicians. On "Coup 2 Gueule," Thiat accuses President Abdoulaye Wade of election fraud and of siphoning money from Senegal's Chemical Industries company (I.C.S.) and the African air traffic management organization (Asecna). He raps in Wolof, the dominant language in Senegal, "Old man, your seven-year presidential reign has been expensive/As if it wasn't enough that you cheated during the last elections/ You ruined the I.C.S. and hijacked Asecna's money." (It flows better in Wolof.)

Most of these rappers made music prior to the political events that swept their countries. But by speaking boldly and openly about a political reality that was not being otherwise acknowledged, rappers hit a nerve, and their music served as a call to arms for the budding protest movements. In Egypt, the rapper Mohamed el Deeb told me in a recent interview, "shallow pop music and love songs got heavy airplay on the radio, but when the revolution broke out, people woke up and refused to accept shallow music with no substance."

Voices of Clarity and Leadership

As the Arab revolutions and African protests are ousting and discrediting establishment politicians, the young populations of these regions are looking to rappers as voices of clarity and leadership. Waterflow raises money at his shows to support his community because, like many of his fans, he believes that "waiting for our political leaders to give us opportunities is a waste of time." Other Senegalese rappers helped found the movement Y'en a Marre ("We're Fed Up"), which has crystallized opposition to President Wade and led a campaign to register young voters for the elections next month. Some are even supporting candidates for president. The rapper Keyti does not back the candidacy of Mr. N'Dour, because he thinks he's trying to run out of self-interest, but acknowledges that it "was much needed to make people realize how politicians have failed."

Rappers are hoping to inaugurate a different kind of politics. They would sooner make a pilgrimage to the South Bronx than to the Senegalese, Sufi holy city of Touba; they reject the predefined roles available within the political arena. And we shouldn't forget that despite being thrust into the spotlight at a historic moment, rappers are also artists who want to make their music. As Deeb raps in his song "Masrah Deeb" (Deeb's Stage)—written in the early days of the Egyptian revolution to remind people why they were taking to the streets—"I'm not a dictator/Deeb's a doctor in the beat department."

American Rap Has Lost Its Political Voice to Apathy

Mark Gunn

Mark Gunn is a radio personality on Magic 101.3 (WMJM) in Louisville, Kentucky, and he occasionally writes for The Voice-Tribune, *a weekly newspaper there.*

This election year [2012] will be a major turning point for the direction of this country.

There are those who want to take the country as far right as far right can go, even at the risk of going over the cliff, and then there's the rest of us.

The last three years of the [Barack] Obama Presidency have brought out the best in some and the worst in others. Ordinary people taking to the streets in protest of inequality on many different levels and politicians hell bent on imposing the very same big government they claim to despise. All of this is going on with a very nasty undercurrent of some of the ugliest racism I've seen from this country in a long time. People have stepped up and taken sides but where is the Hip Hop community?

I find it bitterly ironic that with the election of the nation's first Black President, rappers have been silent. Painfully silent. Why is that? Could it be that the problems facing ordinary Americans, the very same problems that rappers used to give voice to, just don't fit into the "clock dollahs, make it rain at the strip club" mentality that seems to be the latest dumbed down flavor of the month? It's also ironic that an art form that brought about political and social awareness along with a sense of pride has been reduced to so much mental mush. Instead of challenging streams of thought, it grinds the average brain to apathetic pabulum.

I've been around since before Hip Hop went mainstream more than 30 years ago, and as a radio personality, and have seen it grow into a force of good and inspiration. Groups like Public Enemy and Boogie Down Productions led me down the path to a knowledge of self. Artists such as Paris, Kool Moe Dee and X-Clan made it cool to be Pro-Black without being Anti-White by including historical text in their album's liner notes. Songs like "Fight The Power," "Self-Destruction" and countless others not only had a vicious beat. More importantly, they were lyrically potent. Even groups like N.W.A. were important because, as offensive as some found them to be, they had an important message about a side of life that most whites never saw.

Where is that mindset when we need it the most?

The Return of Apathy

The sad irony is that these days people listen to rap more for the beat than they do the actual rhyme.

There are segments of the Tea Party that literally want to rewrite history by removing all references to slavery from school text books. There are those in Arizona that are moving to end any Ethnic Studies classes in a state with a large Latino population. Where is the Hip Hop movement and why are they not speaking out against these atrocities?

Hip Hop stepped up in a major way during the 2008 election and the numbers of younger voters went through the roof. There were those that were apathetic that voted for the first time.

However, instead of keeping a sustained message about the importance of voting and becoming politically active, Hip Hop went back to business as usual: "Glitz, Guns & Girls." It's no surprise that the same apathy that plagued us returned as evidenced by the shamefully low voter turnout in the 2012 midterms. Just think what might have happened if more voters did as James Brown once said, "Get on up. Get into it. Get involved." Why am I so critical of what's happening in Hip Hop? Simple. What was once a powerful force for education and change has become a 21st century version of "Steppin' Fetchit." In order for more young people to become involved, they must be reached in a way they can relate to instead of consuming a non-stop diet of mind-numbing "nincompoopness."

The sad irony is that these days people listen to rap more for the beat than they do the actual rhyme.

Artists Must Be Held Accountable

Today's artists must be made to account for their fundamental lack of respect of the art form and those that came before them. They must be held accountable by parents taking a more active role in what their kids listen to.

We must follow the example of the Occupy protests by Occupying Hip Hop. Speak volumes by withholding your support. You do that through your pocketbook. Choose music by those artists that speak on the important issues of the day instead of the gangsta fairytales weaved in a haze of alcohol and pot.

There are a lot of voices that want to make decisions that will have a great effect on the future. The Hip Hop Generation is a big part of that future. You can either use your voices and talents to speak intelligently about the issues or you can continue the current trend of buffoonery that has no redeeming social value. On second thought, if the best we can get about politics is Wiz Kalifah's "votin' good" quote, I'd rather the Hip Hop community keep its collective mouth shut.

Rap Lyrics Are a Literary Art Form

Alexs Pate

Alexs Pate is an assistant professor of Afro-American and African Studies at the University of Minnesota, where he teaches courses in writing and black literature, including "Poetry of Rap." He is the author of five novels, and his short stories and nonfiction essays have appeared in African American Literary Criticism, Brotherman, Gumbo, After Hours, *and other publications.*

Rap/poetry is and, from all appearances, will continue to be a significant contribution to African American literature. It is a contribution that goes largely unacknowledged, however, because so much attention is focused on the inferior, shallow, simpleminded, and inefficacious rap/poems. It is true, sadly, that a great deal of rap/poetry is caught in a loop, engaged in display and discussion of the basest and lowest standards of life. Ethics, morality, and spirituality are often expressed in terms of acquisition and material gain. Opportunism and accumulation are commonly found in the meanings of some rap/poetry.

Although this art form does have these problems, it still remains the most vibrant element in the landscape of African American literature. This is due in some degree to the sheer quantity of rap/poetry that is produced. It is easy to paint this work with too broad a brush. The good and exemplary get lost in the flurry of profanity, party rhymes, and braggadocio.

But it is also true that there has been no other time in the history of black people in America when they have had access to the technology of artistic production, the technology of distribution, and the willingness to display their unheralded literary capacity. What is remarkable, however, is that this literary capacity erupted in spite of and in defiance of a system of education that does not effectively do its job.

[There is] a way of reading rap/poetry that yields both its contemporary and historical literary value.

Bypassing the System

The elitism of American literary culture, with its agents, editors, and publishers, clearly marginalizes voices that are not from the mainstream. American literary critics, reviewers, agents, and editors, to an alarming degree, know very little about African American literary traditions. Consequently, they do not privilege those traditions and have no interest in their maintenance. I suppose this, too, is largely due to the educational system.

But young developing poets can now bypass that system. And, in so doing, they also escape rigorous reading.... We advocate seeing through the music and the beat of rap—moving beyond the trappings of both true and bogus expressions of hip hop culture—to find the poetry that is there. Once we locate the poetry in rap, we are able to validate it as the sustenance and cultural continuity that poetry provides. In other words, rap/poetry articulates the world that stares back at the rap/poet.

[There is] a way of reading rap/poetry that yields both its contemporary and historical literary value. This way of reading may or may not correspond to any standing literary critical theory, but it does identify a way of reading rap/poetry that encourages the reader to step beyond the dominance of the beat and to see rap/poetry's many dimensions. It is an approach to rap/poetry that allows the reader to make judgments about its construction, its durability, and perhaps even its value. And it is an approach that is based on the components within rap. We have not superimposed a system of critical review but rather looked at rap from the inside out to define its elements.

I believe that nearly every conversation about rap is incomplete and probably specious if rap's literary elements have not been fully considered. To simply bemoan the abstract social implications of rap—to charge it with damaging the black community, for example—without doing the basic tasks of critical reading and comparing and contrasting rap/poems renders all opinions thin. There are too many discussions about rap in which neither proponent or opponent can quote extensively from a variety of rap/poems.

As our capacity to perform these kinds of analytical activities with rap/poetry increases, our conversations about it will become more accurate and more sophisticated.

Reflections of Ourselves

And as we get better about talking about rap—acquiring the ability to distinguish those rap/poems that are outstanding examples of literary and cultural achievement from those that are bad imitations or worse—we will discover that rap/poets (African American, African, white, Asian, Latino, Native American, and all other races and nationalities) have benefited from the literary history and progression of African American literature. We will discover the wide and dynamic range of topics with which these poets engage. We will marvel at the complex and textured images they portray of the people around them and of the life and struggle that encapsulates urban areas. And we will be amazed at the capacity these young poets have to propel us to new understandings about ourselves through their mastery of the parts of speech and their facility with words.

In essence, the heart of the beat—the poetry of rap— provides us with a continuous loop of information and images of ourselves. If you are offended by it, in a way, you should be. The language rap/poets use is the language we use. The images they craft are no different from the ones crafted by screenwriters and crime scene reporters. If their ethics, morals, and values are troubling, it is because of what we have shown them of ourselves. Indeed, we are them.

CHAPTER 2

Is Hip-Hop a Negative Influence on Society?

Overview:
The Hip-Hop Generation

J.D. Gravenor

J.D. Gravenor is a staff writer for The Gazette, *a daily newspaper in Montreal, Canada.*

From living in the friendly neighbourhoods of West Palm Beach, Fla., to some of the toughest parts of north-end St. Michel [a neighborhood in Montreal], Carson Emmanuel has seen a lot in his 17 years. So when something or somebody rubs him the wrong way, he doesn't get mad. He gets even— through rap.

"This week, I had this guy speak my name in a wrong way," the Grade 11 student at Options II High School in Ville Emard [Montreal] said last Thursday [February 2007]. "Now, when somebody doesn't respect you, you know you don't take that too easily. You kind of get ticked off. So I wrote down a quick verse basically saying, 'Don't say anything that would offend me.'"

The exact lyrics are somewhat more explicit. Let's just say that his words are smart, witty and wise, just like the author himself. And if there's one thing Emmanuel has in common with countless teenagers his age, it's his respect for the hip-hop form as a way of dealing with his feelings and identity.

"I would say that hip hop is the main and dominant subculture of youth today," said Jacqueline Celemencki, a graduate student at the Education Department of McGill University. "If you want to know and understand youth culture, you should absolutely be looking at hip hop."

In fact, hip-hop culture is more than just rapping and emceeing. It's a decades-old movement that includes a range of visual and physical expression, like graffiti, urban fashion and breakdancing.

When [one student] talks about hip hop, he singles out the constructive messages it can express.

How Does Hip Hop Shape Identity?

For the past few months, Celemencki has been holding group discussions with Options II students like Emmanuel about how the hip-hop movement shapes their identities and contributes to a sense of who they are. Her research will form the basis for her master's thesis.

Grade 11 student Shaun Polanco-Simmons is one of the members of her group. When he talks about hip hop, he singles out the constructive messages it can express.

"The message can be important," said the 18-year-old. "It can open up my eyes to things I didn't know about the world around me. But I like to hear positive messages, not talking about 'bitches' or 'hos' or 'I've made my money through drugs.' I like hearing about 'I lived my life proper.'"

In addition to the sounds, Polanco-Simmons likes the hip-hop style of graphic art. And while he doesn't wield a spray can, he does like to devote spare time to designing unique and colourful letters throughout his notebooks.

His schoolmate Reilly Duffin, 16, thinks of freestyle writing and rapping as a natural way to express what's on his mind. It also influences his clothing style—which tends to oversized hoodies, ball caps and sneakers.

"Freestyling is not a trick, it's your flow," the Grade 10 student said. "Everybody has a beat to them. Like your heart beat is a consistent thing. So you have that beat in you. The thing is, you just have to trust what's coming out of your mouth. Make sense of it. Make sure it's true.

"Like, I have words in my head. The trouble is putting words together to make sense. As long as I can speak a proper sentence, I can write a rap."

His approach to working is to freestyle while listening to beats of his own or those recorded by friends, or to sounds downloaded from the Internet.

"So whenever I'm just chillin', I just spin a one-two verse on there," he said.

Hip hop has come a long way since the first rappers made their names back in the 1970s—years before Noel Ngoka was born. But as far as the 18-year-old Options II student is concerned, the style and movement has always been there.

Growing Up Hip-Hop

"I've been listening to hip hop since I was a baby," said the Grade 11 student. "It was always in the background, all the time. So I guess we found each other."

While hip hop might be just the ticket for many teens, others can take it or leave it.

The style is a fit for him, because as a downtown resident, he has seen more than his share of rough trade in his day.

"Bums, crackheads, cokeheads, people selling drugs, bums asking for money, all that kind of thing," he said. "Hip hop keeps me out of that. It keeps me motivated."

Like Duffin, it also inspires Ngoka's look: he sports the latest street wear, subtle gold accessories, wraparound shades and tilted ball cap.

"I don't care how people look at me," he said with a winning smile. "As long as I look good in the mirror, I look good on the street."

Kyle Sparks, 16, used to listen to rock and heavy metal, but then his family moved to a different neighbourhood where he was exposed to hip-hop culture.

"I got into rap," said the Grade 10 student. "I started listening to it, started deciphering it, and I started writing it."

Now, he writes verses about everything from crime in the street to the war in Iraq.

"If I see something that I think I should write about or if somebody sparks my interest in a certain topic, then I'll write about it," he said.

Some Teens Opt Out

While hip hop might be just the ticket for many teens, others can take it or leave it.

"I like old school hip hop, but not so much these days," said Grade 11 student Brittany Fisher, 16. "All they talk about is slapping their 'bitches' and making money and selling drugs. And it's not too good. If you watch rap videos, it's all these girls shaking their ass in front of the street. And it's not good for kids watching TV and it's not entertaining. I don't like watching it."

Her classmate, Anessa Kump, 16, more or less agrees.

"I like listening to hip-hop music, but when they call girls 'bitches,' it really brings them down. And I'm not for that," said the Grade 10 student. "It makes the people see girls in a worse way. And young kids these days see rap, and they want to do like the rappers. So then they treat women the way the rappers do and say the words that they say."

Rap Music Is Harmful to African American Communities

E. Faye Williams

E. Faye Williams is the national chairwoman of the National Congress of Black Women, a nonprofit organization dedicated to the educational, political, economic, and cultural development of African American women and their families.

We women, especially we Black women and our children, have been bombarded with misogyny, violence and obscenity through public airwaves day after day. In a society that claims that it is fair and seeks justice for all, too many corporate leaders in the entertainment business have captured the rawness of the feelings of many Black males, and a few Black females, who feel disenfranchised. Some rap music which began with a positive purpose, now taps into the psyche of Black teens who have a sense that no one cares that young Black males are routinely getting the short end of the stick in America. They look at what is happening in the Jena 6 case [six African American teens convicted of beating a white student at Jena High School] in my home state, Louisiana, and they have reason to believe they should be angry with everybody—even with Black women and Black elders who've given their all to try to make life better for them.

Instead of putting adequate funds into the education and care of young people, and the assurance of jobs and a chance to build their own businesses, our system has failed them by steadily diverting funds into war and destruction. We have not

E. Faye Williams, National Congress of Black Women, Testimony before the House Subcommittee on Commerce, Trade and Consumer Protection, Subcommittee on Commerce, Trade and Consumer Protection, "From Imus to Industry: The Business of Stereotypes and Degrading Images," House Committee on Energy and Commerce, United States House of Representatives, September 25, 2007.

always provided the kinds of options that would prevent our young people from idolizing the lives of thugs, pimps, warlords or other negative images. Too many of us have criticized young people for denigrating and disrespecting women and Black people in order to make a living, when they are offered no decent options.

Greed Rules the Airwaves

We have allowed greedy corporate executives—especially those in the entertainment industry—to lead many of our young people to believe that [it] is okay to entertain themselves by destroying the culture of our people. We know all too well what happened to our Native American brothers and sisters in movies through the years. The profanity, vulgarity, and obscenity we see and hear today have become commonplace to the point of being genocidal.

We believe in freedom of speech, but with every right goes responsibility.

Even our very young babies have become subjected to horrifying language and images on public airwaves by those who should know better, but are claiming that this is the only way to relate to our children. If you haven't seen the so-called public service advertisement that looks like just another cartoon, called *Read a Book*, you need to see it to understand what I am talking about. What are teachers to do when they hear these children repeat these words?

Why should our children be assaulted daily with garbage under the guise of First Amendment rights that say nothing about responsibility?

The corporate executives that lure our young people into believing it is all right to destroy the culture of a people seem to have targeted Black women and our families who've contributed so much to this nation. The same can be said historically about our Native American sisters and their families.

We believe in freedom of speech, but with every right goes responsibility. We have a right to earn money, but we have a corresponding responsibility to pay income taxes.

Rights and Responsibilities

We have a right to travel on public transportation such as airplanes, but a responsibility not to carry on or even mention guns or other weapons while riding. We have a right to have children, but a responsibility not to abuse or neglect them. . . .

Using the public airwaves may be a right, but the line must be drawn and balanced by the responsibility to refrain from painting an immoral image of an entire race of people—and of Black women in particular. Not only entertainment executives, but advertisers must act more responsibly. Why should we want to buy a product that pays for our destruction?. . .

Those who use the public airwaves must be made to understand that there are consequences for those who insist upon subjecting our children to songs like *Read a Book*. The words are too bizarre to mention in this hearing, but it's easy enough to hear them on the Internet or on television.

When you see the video and hear the words, you will understand why we are so highly disturbed about what is brought to our children—while those who bring it castigate those of us who object to it. We all want our children to read a book, but our children are not so dumb that they need to be told in such vile and bizarre language to do so.

Along with the right of freedom of speech goes the responsibility not to bombard those airwaves with filthy, derogatory, offensive, indecent language that crosses the line of decency and shocks the conscience of all who hear or see it. We're not objecting to what goes on in adult clubs here; we're talking about what is brought to our children, who deserve better images.

A Misrepresentation of Culture

Nearly 15 years ago, my predecessor, the late Dr. C. DeLores Tucker, warned us about where we were headed when we allow unrestricted rights to spew vicious, hateful words about women, and how this contributes to violence and disrespect. The results have come to pass.

On occasion, we turn our televisions on and we are embarrassed and humiliated to see so many Black men and women portrayed as gangsters, pimps, prostitutes, and thugs—with no mention of the great works of our people—no balance what-so-ever.

Many Black men and women serve this country with honor and distinction, and deserve better treatment.

What we so often see on television, videos and elsewhere is not the culture of the people I know. It's not the culture of the majority of Black people. Our culture has more to do with respecting our elders, our sisters, our mothers and grandmothers—but where are those images? In our culture, the gangster is the exception; the thug is the exception; the pimp is the exception; the prostitute is the exception. Many Black men and women serve this country with honor and distinction, and deserve better treatment.

Black women have served this country as Surgeon General, Secretary of Labor, Energy, Housing and Urban Development, Secretary of State, in Congress, as Diplomats, as college Presidents, in law, medicine and all walks of life—and too rarely do we even hear many of our public officials speak out about balancing rights with responsibilities when it comes to the images portrayed of Black women and our families on public airwaves.

Double Standard Is Unacceptable

[Radio personality] Don Imus was wrong when he belittled the young women at Rutgers. Courtland Milloy of the *Washington Post* is usually right on the issues, but he just plain got it wrong when he belittled our efforts to demand better images of women and our families in our "Enough is Enough" campaign. Isiah Thomas is wrong when he says that it's highly offensive for a white male to call a Black female a bitch, but it's okay for a Black man to do so. Well, Mr. Thomas would be surprised to know that they're equally offensive and totally unacceptable to Black women. . . .

We in the Women's Coalition for Dignity and Diversity respect the First Amendment rights of every citizen. We believe in the right to free speech, but we also believe in decent speech.

Yes, rights without responsibilities should be labeled anarchy; yet that is much of what we see and hear on our public airwaves. It's time for Congress to stand up and insist upon responsibility, and make it clear to the FCC and the FTC what their roles should be in making it happen. That is what we in the Women's Coalition for Dignity and Diversity are saying.

We can't, and we won't, sit around and wait for *gangsta rap* and other vicious media images of us to self destruct. We're not just talking about BET, and its parent company, Viacom, about bombardment of our community with vicious images of women and of Black people. We call upon all media to be more responsible. We also call upon advertisers to be more sensitive to the pain these negative images cause those of us being targeted.

Fifteen Years of Campaigning Against Rap

I conclude by repeating what President Lyndon Johnson once said, "How incredible it is that in this fragile existence we should hate and destroy one another!", and I say that without responsibility, that is exactly what happens to women and our families each time someone decides to denigrate us on public airwaves for the almighty dollar, and in the name of free speech.

Being credited *with*, or being blamed *for*, the diminishing sales of *gangsta rap* and offensive language and images is a banner we proudly wear; but it's not happening because we *allowed* it to self destruct. It's happening because we've been intent upon making it happen for years—at least since the National Congress of Black Women began our campaign nearly 15 years ago, with others joining us recently. . . .

We need the Progressives, Conservatives, Democrats, Republicans, Independents, and all others to talk not just about rights of free speech, but also about the responsibilities inherent in this great freedom.

Girls Are Especially Vulnerable to Hip-Hop's Hypersexual Message

Beatrice Koehler-Derrick

Beatrice Koehler-Derrick is a writer based in New York City. This selection was originally published in Home Girls Make Some Noise: Hip Hop Feminist Anthology, *a collection of hip-hop feminist writings.*

"You girls done in there?" I push the pink linoleum door open a crack, catching a whiff of stagnant number two, generic air freshener and not enough ventilation. La'Nyce, Bryanna and Catherine are too busy judging who can shake their butts the fastest to notice their Kinder Camp counselor peeking at them. I clear my throat. Bryanna turns and looks at me. She flashes a sugary smile mid-"pop"; her hands are on her knees, her butt sticks up against the wall. La'Nyce looks scared. She's afraid I'll tell her mommy. Catherine raises the corner of her upper lip and rolls her eyes, obviously disgusted that I interrupted their fun.

"What? Ms. Bea, we're just dancing!" says Bry-Bry.

"And what are you *supposed* to be doing?" I ask sternly, gesturing toward the stalls while trying to hold back laughter. After a calm afternoon of peeling pieces of macaroni and cheese off table tops and slowly spelling words needed to complete homework assignments, walking in on this competition was the wake-up I needed.

The girls are five and six years old. They wear their hair in ball-balls, and survive off a strict diet of cheddar Gold Fish and candy. With an unhampered boldness, they will tell you if you're getting fat, flirting too much or have a large zit on your face with the casualty of a considerate by-stander informing you that your shirt tag is out. In many ways my job has made me more confrontational, but these "Toddlers Gone Wild" definitely caught me off guard. Pairs of miniature Mary Janes kick at the air, suspended between tile floor and stall, as I scratch my head and try to compose the talk all of us know is coming.

Time for a Talk

Up until this point, the role of rap music has always remained minimal in our classroom; something to power our games of musical chairs, a station to play on a beat-up boom box during swimming time on Thursdays. However, Catherine, Bryanna and La'Nyce utilized rap music in a new way when they held this competition in private. Though there was no stereo in the girls' bathroom, I wonder what songs were playing in their heads. What lyrics were they mouthing the words to? I'd noticed the way La'Nyce was seductively glancing behind her bony shoulder, an invisible male counterpart seemingly encouraging her to shake a little faster. As a woman who loves and embraces hip-hop, but is disappointed by the industry's overwhelmingly misogynistic portrayal of females, how do I address these students of mine?

Up until this point, the role of rap music has always remained minimal in our classroom; something to power our games of musical chairs.

I sit the girls down on the edge of the wooden cubbies that line the hall. Taking a crouching position opposite them, I search for a way to get this conversation going.

"Would you do that in front of your mommies?" I ask.

The girls all shake their heads.

"Are you going to tell on us?" Catherine asks hesitantly.

"No, not this time. But you know there's a reason why your mommies wouldn't be very happy to hear about this. At five and six years old, you shouldn't be concerned about doing dances that older teenagers and grownups do at the club." I sigh. I'm obviously not sure enough of my own opinions to get into a long sermon.

> *I found myself growing increasingly disgusted with the message ... the film was sending and ... how well it was being received.*

"Listen," I said, "I don't want that going on any more here, you understand? It's not cute. It's not appropriate. And it's not something for little girls like you to be doing." The accused release a breath of relief, and assure me it won't happen again, scurrying into the classroom, already chattering about who can jump double-dutch better. I feel like a failure. These girls love rap stars so it makes sense that they imitate the women who surround them in most videos. Even though their mothers have established that "poppin'" and "twurkin'" are moves that are too fresh for girls their age, dancing provocatively is fun, even thrilling, to my students. I had interrupted their session, chided and threatened them about continuing this behavior, but how had I helped them question their own motives?

What I wanted to teach them was that dancing like "video honeys" wasn't the only way to get attention from the men they admire. I should have discussed what made them look up to background dancers; encouraged them to truly examine the images they were presented with. What I lacked, besides *cajones*, was a broad selection of emerging female artists in hip-hop to recommend my girls: rappers whose flow covered a variety of emotions and topics; ladies whose dance was passionate and guiltless, not just [a] job to get bills paid. That night, I walked home past a liquor store displaying butts for Bacardi and breast for Budweiser: the models' hardened gaze followed me for blocks. Their eyes seemed frighteningly familiar.

Hustle and Flow

Back in the heart of the Midwest, I went to see Craig Brewer's *Hustle & Flow*, a movie about a pimp who wants to become a rap star and uses both the moral and financial support of his hos to help him succeed. During the hour and a half spent in the dark, cool, theater, I found myself growing increasingly disgusted with the message I felt the film was sending and probably even more disturbed by how well it was being received. One of the pimp's hos works at a strip club where several of the girls make their butts "clap" for the camera. *The male moviegoers cheer with enthusiasm.* Nola, the pimp's number one doe-eyed prostitute, endures backseat sex sessions in hundred-degree heat when she is reassured that "things will get better soon." *The audience sends supportive smiles up at the screen.* Her pimp's progress toward becoming a rap star is slightly delayed when he ends up in jail, but Nola puts on a mini-skirted business suit, implying that she's ready to suck a couple of DJ d**** if it will get her man on the air. *Nods of approval from the twelve year olds in the row in front of me.*

Shug, a pregnant prostitute, is equally "down for the cause" when she's asked to sing the hook to a couple songs on her pimp's record. She belts out lyrics that express how hard it is for a pimp to pay rent, put gas in the car and keep his bitches satisfied. Even though these songs show the perspective of her rapper, and do nothing to express hers, Shug is shown teary-eyed and thankful, expressing her utmost appreciation for this singing opportunity. It was enough that he arranged the sale of her body in ways she could never do for *herself*, but now, a chance to serenade the world with songs boasting about how skillful he is at his job! What an opportunity!

Hustle & Flow reconfirmed the way people in that movie theater view women in hip-hop: useful only when they are singing or looking sexy to increase revenue. Would I have been as upset with the movie if there were more options presented for women in the hip-hop industry?

Dae-Dae liked the attention she got when she rapped rough, and I could relate.

Working with the kids at the Youth Center had demonstrated another option for women in the rap world. I'd been sitting in front of six-year-old Dae-Dae, a new girl to Kinder Camp, who was determined to beat me in our freestyle battle. Much like the girls I caught in the bathroom, Dae-Dae was a pro at mimicking what she saw and admired, but the women in hip-hop she chose to look up to were those who focused less on their physical attractiveness and more on their lyrics. These women used their hard-hitting lines to get people's attention, expecting necks to turn in shock after hearing "masculine" things come out of feminine lips.

Kid Rap

I had just finished rapping a little bit for our class, when Dae-Dae strutted over and challenged me, ready to show the rest of the kids her talent. I pounded out a beat on the table, the abandoned arts and crafts pieces bouncing wildly as their constructors gathered around us.

"You ain't nobody and you shoes are dirty/you couldn't spell if your mommy whispered to you/ you like to eat doggie do-do/ I'm the best/ what is this?"

She popped my collar, stood back with her arms folded, and mugged me, her bright green "I [heart] JESUS" barrettes swinging in front of her eyes. The rest of the crowd "oooed" and "ahhhhed." My co-workers were on the ground dying of laughter. Dae-Dae cracked a little bit of a smile, but she was obviously very serious. I remembered grinning and telling her there was no way I could think of a comeback. She rapped more for me later, after everyone had returned to work. Her little forehead scrunched up as she spit lines about stabbing things, throwing punches at people's faces and strangling a cat. While I could tell her anger was real, it was obvious she didn't really intend to do these things. She wasn't sure what made her mad, or couldn't find the words to express why. Dae-Dae liked the attention she got when she rapped rough, and I could relate.

I can't help but wish a new generation of women in hip-hop would emerge.

I used to come up with battle lyrics that echoed the same gory lines I heard my male friends spit. I'd rock a hoodie and hat to football games and, at halftime, hope to break everyone's expectations of what a girl was capable of rapping about. Hip-hop was cathartic. I'd channel all my "teenage angst" into stories of murder and poverty that were not mine. But as the crowd egged me on, my topics became a part of me: something essential to my flow. As I grew up, and puberty hit, my tomboy clothes were somewhat reluctantly replaced by more form fitting jeans and tops. Still into rap, I was shocked but pleased by the reaction I received from my newfound curves. Violent rhymes were replaced by me bragging about how much money I made and how good in bed I was, although I probably had all of ten dollars at home, and was about as sexually experienced as a box of hair. At sixteen, though, it felt right; it felt like me. From hustling bravado to hustling sex appeal, my style of rapping was evolving along with my body.

Mixed Emotions

When watching music videos, five-year-old Dae-Dae dreams of being invited by her favorite rapper to spit a few bars in his new video. She feels the hot studio lights beating down on her face. He sways with her to the beat, encouraging the audience to listen to what she was saying by mouthing "Ooooh" at how tight her flow is. Seventeen-year-old Dae-Dae might have different ambitions. Would she want the rapper to circle her toned body, wordlessly appreciating her thickness with his eyes, his teeth biting lower lip, drawing the viewers' attention to her physical assets instead of her lyrical ones? Which would I prefer? At the time that I worked with the kids in Harlem I hadn't, and still haven't, found the answer to that question.

It's tempting to badmouth the women in short shorts and stilettos who dance sexually for rapper-revenue. I've scoffed at these video girls before, but a part of me wants to be just like them: sexy and desirable and not concerned, at least for the moment, with coming across as "consciously-minded" or "deep." For all my efforts to be viewed as politically aware and correct, I don't want to be invisible to the opposite sex.

While searching for balance within myself, I can't help but wish a new generation of women in hip-hop would emerge (and get love from record companies) who could break the current unwritten rap code of conduct—hustle or be hustled. Women who know what kind of attention they want to receive from men as artists and members of the "fairer sex." Ladies who don't need a perfectly built body to get people to notice them. Lyricists who don't need to mimic men to get listeners to take heed of their words.

Hopes for Women Role Models

I want Catherine, La'Nyce and Bryanna to be more than eye-candy who "bend over and wiggle with it" to get props from the rapper: I want them to imitate dancers who choreograph, teach and truly pour their souls into the art of dance. I want to watch the reactions of an audience viewing a film on the financially successful woman MCs who write innovative or controversial material. I want Dae-Dae to grow up hearing a woman with less hustle, more flow: a chick who raps about everything from pantyhose and pumps to those days when you just want to chill in your sweat pants, from club hoppin' and enjoying looks from sexy men to knowing your worth as a woman and leaving a man if he becomes abusive.

I try to picture the girls I worked with in Harlem as they get older. I can almost see what would happen if we all re-united at the Youth Center years from now. The same little girls who used to hug me around the knees will proudly in-troduce me to their own toddlers. After a makeshift game of musical chairs and too much Kool-Aid, the women will bring their diaper bags and squirming children into the same girls' bathroom they used so many years ago. As the pink linoleum door is swinging closed, I'll overhear laughter as they debate who was the ass-shaking princess back in the day. While they attempt to set the record straight using new moves, someone will hit a beat on the changing table. The sound of their tal-ent, their flow, will reach the ears of those who want to listen: too precious, even in its imperfections, to stay in the back-ground.

Rap Has the Potential to Expose Social Injustice

Jeff Chang

Jeff Chang is a journalist and music critic. His writing has appeared in such publications as Spin, Vibe, *and* Mother Jones.

Jerry Quickley, hip-hop poet, performance artist, and war correspondent, has seen hell. It is a post-"liberated"Baghdad street, jammed with beat-up Brazilian and Czech sedans spewing trails of carbon monoxide, clouds of dust thickening in the 125-degree heat. He is riding shotgun in an Iraqi friend's car. "You have no traffic lights because there's no electricity," he says. "You have no police because they'd just be shot or blown up. You can barely breathe." U.S. soldiers fire into the air to clear traffic and scare off would-be bombers, and Iraqi drivers ram into each other as they scramble to get out of the way. "And while this is all going on," Quickley says, "this friend of mine is playing songs by 50 Cent."

The top-selling do-ragged and body-oiled rapper—whose smash debut was entitled *Get Rich or Die Tryin'* and whose 2005 album *The Massacre* occasioned a book, a feature movie, a bloody video game, a bling-encrusted line of watches, shoe and "enhanced water" endorsements, not to mention tabloid headlines about a beef with a former protégé culminating in real-life shootings—warbles through the busted car stereo in a nasal drawl: "Many men wish death upon me."

"Sartre was right," thought Quickley. "This is *No Exit*."

For many, this is what hip-hop has become: an omnipresent, grisly, übermacho soundtrack. Don Imus unleashed the latest hip-hop backlash when he noted that in calling the Rut-

gers women's basketball team "nappy-headed hos" he was using an argot popularized by rappers. The frenzy of finger-
pointing that followed culminated with the spectacle of Bill
O'Reilly lecturing hip-hop advocates on sexism and the "n-
word" while Oprah berated Russell Simmons and other industry executives.

The talk show circus aside, there's plenty of evidence that
people are weary of corporate rap. Only 59 million rap albums were sold in the United States last year, down from 90
million in 2001. According to a University of Chicago study,
most youths—whether black, white, or Hispanic—believe that
rap videos portray women of color in a negative light. Once a
cacophony of diverse voices, the genre now looks like a monoculture whose product, like high-fructose corn syrup, is de-
signed not to nourish but simply to get us hooked on other
products, from McDonald's to Courvoisier.

---

*Hip-hop-based community groups have recharged the so-
cial justice movement and launched get-out-the-vote
campaigns in neighborhoods most candidates and parties
wouldn't touch.*

Quickley, though, remains a true believer in hip-hop's
transformational potential. For him, it goes back to the summer of 1976, three years before the Sugarhill Gang's break-
through hit "Rapper's Delight." He was 12 and sitting on a
scorching NYC stoop when someone popped in a cassette tape
featuring a DJ mixing up bombastic rhythms on two turntables. It rocked his young world. He started visiting block
parties to hear DJs spin and rappers rap, and soon learned
how to mix. He jumped the subway turnstiles and became a
graffiti bomber. After poetry overtook doodling in his sketch-
books, he became a rapper.

To Quickley and to millions of others, the new genre's appeal was visceral. It was a true counterculture, skirting legality

and authority with a smirk. It broke down social barriers. DJs mixed Led Zeppelin and Aerosmith with James Brown and the Meters. By the mid-'80s hip-hop looked like the most significant youth movement since the '60s. It expanded beyond the original "four elements"—rap, DJing, graffiti writing, and b-boying (also known, incorrectly, as break dancing)—into virtually every art form and became the lingua franca [common language] for an increasingly connected, polycultural world.

Back then, "media assassin" and Public Enemy collaborator Harry Allen coined the phrase "hip-hop activism" to describe the movement's potential to spur social change. But as industry execs began to capitalize on hip-hop's popularity, its renegade spirit was largely suppressed by displays of conspicuous consumption and gratuitous machismo.

But now, with the industry on the ropes and the political sphere energized, the transformative power of hip-hop may finally be reemerging. Over the past decade, hip-hop-based community groups have recharged the social justice movement and launched get-out-the-vote campaigns in neighborhoods most candidates and parties wouldn't touch. (Full disclosure: I have been active in two of these groups, serving on the board of the League of Young Voters and organizing for the National Hip-Hop Political Convention.) Even moguls such as Jay-Z, Simmons, and Sean "P. Diddy" Combs have thrown their weight behind voter outreach. And while the results are hard to track case by case, one massive shift is undeniable: In 2004, half of the 4 million new voters under 30 were people of color—a demographic watershed largely overlooked by the media.

"It's one of the wonders of the world that this little neighborhood thing, that when I started vibing on it was maybe 10,000 kids running around the city, has completely changed the face of the planet," Quickley says. "All the corporations and commercial interests try to tell you otherwise, but I've seen it go down like that in my lifetime."

Bronx Beats to Suburban Streets

Hip-hop began in the Bronx, a borough ripped in two by Robert Moses' Cross-Bronx Expressway. Stranded by deindustrialization, half the Bronx's white residents fled; the borough was left for dead by city officials. Slumlording and arson reduced housing stock by four blocks a week. In the abandoned tenements, gangs replaced families.

But an unprecedented 1971 gang peace treaty unleashed the creative explosion that became known as hip-hop. It didn't start out as an explicitly political movement—more like a set of pastimes poor kids devised to celebrate their survival. They spray-painted aliases on walls and subways, rapped Jamaican-style over funky Afro-Latin-influenced groove records, and danced to the percussive breaks. "To go from running down the block to escape a gang to being able to walk any block freely, that's one of the greatest joys," says Tony Tone, a gang member who quit and became part of the pioneering rap group the Cold Crush Brothers. "Hip-hop saved a lot of lives."

As with rock and roll a generation before, being attacked by a bunch of parents was the quickest way for hip-hop to gain cred with a wider audience of kids.

This Bronx scene spread across the country, remixed and revitalized in each community, and by the late '80s, hip-hop was articulating an emerging post-civil rights worldview. Rap artists like Chuck D and KRS-ONE spotlighted the effects of crack and violence on inner-city youths and openly questioned why black community leaders were neither addressing these urgent issues nor mentoring young leaders. Carmen Ashhurst was a filmmaker who, in 1988, went to work for Def Jam cofounder Russell Simmons (whose brother is DJ Run from RUN D.M.C.). To her, the motivation to switch genres was clear: "Getting control of our images," she says. "This was young people who at that time weren't being listened to by anybody. Rap became a de facto voice of black America." Or, more accurately, voices. A 1991 Public Enemy tour included acts as disparate as L.A. gangsta pioneer Ice T, style maestros A Tribe Called Quest, and future actors Queen Latifah and Will Smith.

By then, every pundit and politician had an opinion about rap, whether they'd listened to it or not. Some commentators valued rap's truth-telling, but not all understood its s***-talking. Battle-rhyming-boasting about yourself and denigrating your competitor—has been a source of vitality and innovation for the genre. And as far back as the Sugarhill Gang, the braggadocio included brand-name dropping and talk of having "more money than a sucker could ever spend"; there was always an aspirational aspect to this poetry born of poverty.

But songs like N.W.A.'s 1988 "F--- tha Police"—a prescient condemnation of the racist LAPD—scared people. In the wake of the 1992 L.A. riots, a rising tide of anti-rap sentiment cohered into a full-blown culture war as conservatives like Bob Dole joined Tipper Gore, civil rights leaders like C. Delores Tucker, and key Democrats like Carol Moseley-Braun and Joe Lieberman in an alliance to stamp out so-called "gangsta rap." Lobbies like the Fraternal Order of Police and the National Rifle Association forced record labels to drop "politically sensitive" acts like Paris, Kool G. Rap, and Intelligent Hoodlum.

The plan backfired completely. As with rock and roll a generation before, being attacked by a bunch of parents was the quickest way for hip-hop to gain cred with a wider audience of kids. By 1995, rap was one of music's best-selling genres.

For entrepreneurs like Simmons, rap's new crossover appeal represented an enormous business opportunity. "He sold the concept to the mainstream that hip-hop was a lifestyle, not just a music," says Ashhurst, who became president of Def Jam in 1990. By 1999, Simmons sold his share of Def Jam to concentrate on "the urban aspirational lifestyle" market, where, he told me, "there's always room for growth."

The Rap Monoculture

As hip-hop became a big business, the major labels went on a buying spree, making instant fortunes for indie-minded artist/ entrepreneurs like Percy "Master P" Miller, Earl "E-40" Stevens, Bryan "Baby" Williams, and Shawn "Jay-Z" Carter. But the passage of the 1996 Telecommunications Act massively increased economies of scale and put pressure on companies to reduce risk. Six major labels merged into four, laid off hundreds of employees, and sharply narrowed the range of voices, styles, and stories with access to global distribution. At the same time, radio giants like Clear Channel limited playlists, video and radio budgets skyrocketed, and payola thrived.

By embracing the image of black men as oversexed thugs, corporate rap perpetuates age-old stereotypes.

The rich boil of rhyme spinners, sweet-tongued slick talkers, streetwise corner boys, high-minded race men and women, my-block griots, kente-clothed Afrocentrists, and chest-thumping Alis gave way to a bland array of hosts and hostesses for the Bling Shopping Network. Corporate hip-hop's monoculture made icons of synergy-friendly male acts, pushed women back to the margins, and shut out emerging gay and lesbian voices completely. If it wasn't "Gin and Juice" or "Baby Got Back," it didn't get corporate love. "It's really gotten to the point where the only acceptable public image for young black men is some variation on thuggery," says Ashhurst, who quit the music industry in 1996 over its rising tide of sexism and violence and is now writing a memoir called *Selling My Brothers*.

Paul Porter, cofounder of the media-justice think tank Industry Ears, saw these changes firsthand as BET's hip-hop video program director. "We used to see the same storyboard of sex, drugs, rims, and attitude," he says. "We used to vote out some of these videos all the time, and up to 2000, there was a point when we used to blur out champagne bottles. And then it came down to the line where—I'll never forget when [then-BET owner] Bob Johnson called me—this is 1999—I was having some issues with Def Jam executives, and he said, 'Play the video. Def Jam spent $3 million. Just play the video.' And that's when I knew it had gone haywire." As Jay-Z, who is now Def Jam's CEO, famously rapped, "I dumb down for my audience and double my dollars. They criticize me for it, yet they all yell 'Holla.'"

In *Beyond Beats & Rhymes*, documentary filmmaker Byron Hurt's "loving critique" of hip-hop's misogyny and homophobia (which aired on PBS), Hurt asks unsigned rappers gathered outside an industry event to audition for him. Their cliched battle rhymes are predictably bloody, sexist, and homophobic. When Hurt challenges them, they lament that this is the only rap that gets record deals. "The expectations are so well known that the artists conform to them," says Hurt.

As Hurt notes, by embracing the image of black men as oversexed thugs, corporate rap perpetuates age-old stereotypes. There is, Simmons acknowledges, "a streak of negativity on the part of some executives. There are some opportunities for short-term success on stereotypical ideas. But that shakes itself out. Artificial artists lose their footing."

Porter is less optimistic. "If this is the only thing the public hears, that's what they're gonna want," he says. "It's common sense. If McDonald's is on every corner, eventually you go into a McDonald's. Don't tell me that because it sells, it's good. Crack sells."

Superpredators to Super Tuesday

What created the dominance of "thug rap"? Was it rappers "keeping it real," a cynical industry, or the politics of fear? It's worth noting that the hip-hop generation came of age as America's attitudes toward urban youths morphed from "benign neglect" to "lock 'em all up." It was John Dilulio, President George W. Bush's first director of Faith-Based and Community Initiatives, who argued in the early 1990s that rising numbers of youths of color meant Americans would be facing a generation of "superpredators." Juvenile crime was well on its way to historical lows, but politicians on both sides of the aisle raced to pass draconian policies that packed prisons and jails with small-time drug and "anti-loitering" offenders. Is it any wonder that thuggery sold?

Some of the most interesting work in hip-hop politics has been done at the local level, where militant skepticism and passionate pragmatism have quietly built a network of visionary, rough-and-ready organizations.

If government seemed to be writing off young people, they responded in kind. After helping to elect Bill Clinton in 1992, the year of Rock the Vote, youth turnout plunged. This has been misread as apathy. But a growing body of evidence suggests otherwise. Rates of volunteerism and activism are twice as high among those under 25 as they are among boomers. In 2006, a longitudinal national survey of college freshmen run by UCLA found that half of those polled had participated in a demonstration during the past year—three times more than in '66, at the peak of the civil rights movement. And that University of Chicago study found that a majority of today's black and Hispanic youths felt that government cared very little about them. Yet more than three in four also believed they could make a difference by participating in politics.

And in 2004, they did. Together, Simmons' Hip-Hop Summit Action Network and P. Diddy's Citizen Change Campaign, grassroots groups like the National Hip-Hop Political Convention and League of Young Voters, and a number of anti-Bush and antiwar hip-hop anthems and videos by artists ranging from Kanye West to Eminem all urged youths to vote. Exit polls documented 4 million new voters under 30, the biggest youth surge since the voting age was lowered to 18 in 1972. More than half were people of color. Similar polls in 2006 confirmed these trends. What's more, in '06 voters under 30 went Democratic by a nearly 3-to-2 margin. The numbers weren't the result of concentrated party efforts like, say, Karl Rove's work with evangelical voters. In fact, not until after the elections did Democratic strategists Peter Leyden and Ruy Teixeira gush in a white paper that 18- to 24-year-olds at the tip of an 80-million-strong "millennial" boomlet are "an enormous asset for progressives going forward."

From Oakland to Newark, hip-hop organizations are taking on the old issues of poverty and gun violence.

Big electoral trends aside, some of the most interesting work in hip-hop politics has been done at the local level, where militant skepticism and passionate pragmatism have quietly built a network of visionary, rough-and-ready organizations. The most innovative—such as Boston's Youth Organizing Project, Brooklyn's Malcolm X Grassroots Movement, Chicago's Southwest Youth Collaborative/University of Hip-Hop, Cincinnati's Elementz, and Selma's 21st Century Youth Leadership Project—blur the lines between politics and culture, using art, dance, rap production, or turntablism to leverage kids into fierce political action.

As Jakada Imani of Oakland's Ella Baker Center for Human Rights notes, "Hip-hop is primarily about reshaping the world in our image. It's the same in social change. That means figuring out how to tell the truth and get heads to nod at the same time."

In the past five years, hip-hop organizers have stopped construction of juvenile detention facilities in California and New York City, helped can environmental deregulation legislation in New Mexico, passed a college debt-forgiveness initiative in Maine, created networks for Katrina survivors across the South, and helped elect dozens of local candidates. Organizations such as Oakland's Youth Media Council and New York City's R.E.A.C.Hip-Hop and hip-hop pioneer Afrika Bambaataa's Balance the Airwaves Campaign have prodded radio monopolies such as Clear Channel and Emmis Communications to play more local music and feature more progressive voices. After convincing the city of Oakland to fund a Green Job Corps training program for inner-city youths, the Ella Baker Center got Rep. Hilda Solis (D-Calif.) and Nancy Pelosi to insert language into a House energy bill creating a $25 million Green Jobs Act.

And from Oakland to Newark, hip-hop organizations are taking on the old issues of poverty and gun violence. In Milwaukee, where 28 shootings were reported last Memorial Day alone, the three-year-old hip-hop organization Campaign Against Violence deals with these demons every day; a brother of one of the organizers was killed in late 2006.

"Milwaukee is so much further down the [conservative] path than other cities," says the campaign's 29-year-old political director Rob "Biko" Baker. "They got rid of welfare here first. They privatized schools here first. On the coasts, there are still resources; there's a professionalization of the organizing. Here it's just straight raw and uncut. So what do we do so that people don't die?"

Milwaukee officials have mostly offered more tough-on-crime measures. By contrast, the campaign, which has a staff of 7 and a volunteer force of 20, has trained thousands of youths in conflict resolution. Key to its work are poetry workshops in schools and juvenile detention facilities, where kids are asked to complete the sentences "The truth is. . ." and

"Where I'm from. . ." They then read their answers aloud to each other—"The truth is I don't want to go to jail" or "Where I'm from people get killed."

"After they release that," says 31-year-old education director Carey "C.J." Jenkins, "they're ready for the business. They're ready to organize."

By combining "soft" cultural work and "hard" door-to-door organizing, the campaign has built a sizable base. When police officers were acquitted in the brutal beating of a biracial man in 2004, its protests helped make it a federal case. In 2006, the group turned out 15,000 mostly first-time voters. Recently, Wisconsin governor Jim Doyle made the campaign's proposal to close a loophole used by unlicensed gun dealers the centerpiece of his anticrime initiative.

"Organizing the community, it's really not so much about votes," says Jenkins, who himself never voted before getting involved with the campaign in 2005. "It's about maturity and understanding that politics play a part in your everyday life."

Hip-Hop Is Dead; Long Live Hip-Hop

In 2006, when Nas released *Hip-Hop Is Dead*, no rap albums were among the year's top 10 best-sellers. Former BET executive Porter says, "I blame the record companies. They're sticking with the same formula. Hip-hop's 30 years old now, and they've been stuck on stupid for 10 years." In the wake of the Imus debacle, Simmons and Dr. Ben Chavis of the Hip-Hop Summit Action Network called a meeting of industry big shots to address sexism in rap. Gathered at the home of Warner Music Group head Lyor Cohen, the execs couldn't reach consensus—some worried about censorship, others wanted to let the issue blow over—so a week later, Chavis and Simmons called for a voluntary ban on [the "n word"] and ["b**ch."] That wasn't enough to stop a new round of congressional hearings, though Rep. Bobby Rush (D-Ill.), the former Black Panther who called for them, said he was hoping not to use "regulatory solutions." By the end of the summer, the rap game seemed somehow more . . . civil. When 50 Cent first heard that Kanye West's record was dropping the same day as his, he did make threats—but only to quit the game. And by September the two were sharing a Rolling Stone cover; blogs circulated pictures of them hugging after the photo shoot. And if hip-hop activists emerged in part to scream at their elders, now they seem eager to collaborate. "Young people certainly need to be at the forefront of any movement," says Nicole Lee, political director of the Ella Baker Center. "But we can't do it by ourselves. Any movement for peace has to have reconciliation as a core commitment. We're making a shift from the politics of complaint to the politics of possibility."

Can hip-hop grow into its potential? Can rap sell activism as well as it has $150 sneakers, bottle service, and grill work? Can the very people who've made vast fortunes off selling stupid help reform the industry? "The thing I love about hip-hop," says Chavis, "is that it is evolutionary."

American Rap Can Promote Political Empowerment

Lester Spence

Lester Spence is an associate professor of political science at Johns Hopkins University and the author of Stare in the Darkness: The Limits of Hip-hop and Black Politics.

On January 20, 2009, at 4:30 a.m., with three close friends and my oldest daughter, I was at the Mall in Washington, D.C. We had traveled from Baltimore on only three hours of sleep to see Barack Obama inaugurated as the 44th president of the United States. That morning, the five of us stood in the bitter cold for several hours, waiting for the sun to come up. Then waited hours more for the ceremony. I had never attended an inauguration before. I had never even watched one on television. But this was too important to pass up. More people were on the Mall for Obama's inauguration than for any other event in Washington's history. And I've seen pictures of people watching the ceremony in places as far away as Kenya and the Middle East. This reflects a belief that Obama represents the best hope for political change, particularly given the current economic crisis. And the significance of Obama's election for racial politics is undeniable. No other industrialized nation has ever elected a member of its most subjugated racial minority to its highest office.

And this fact raises a critical question: What confluence of events made Obama's election (and his wide margin of victory) possible?

As a scholar of American politics, I can point to traditional political factors. For the majority of the last eight years, the Republican Party has controlled the executive, legislative, and judicial branches. And those eight years have been remarkably bad for America, domestically and internationally. Given the record of GOP control during these years (think Hurricane Katrina, the war in Iraq, the current housing crisis), it was easy for voters to vote retrospectively, to look at the past eight years as representative of GOP control and vote another way.

Why, for the first time, did people feel comfortable casting a vote for a black man with the middle name of Hussein?

But this only explains the ascendance of the Democratic Party, *not* the ascendance of Barack Obama.

It bears repeating: Not only had the United States never elected as president a man not defined as "white" by the census, but no other industrialized nation had ever done anything close. What explains Obama's election? Why, for the first time, did people feel comfortable casting a vote for a black man with the middle name of Hussein?

What Made Obama's Campaign Different?

We could turn to the standard answers. Perhaps campaign commercials painting his opponent, Senator John McCain, as out of touch did it. Perhaps voters saw McCain during the debate and were loath to cast a ballot for someone they perceived to be too old for the job. Perhaps the money that Obama raised simply overpowered his opponent. But each of these standard answers misses something. Why was Obama able to raise so much money given his race? What happened to give white voters the ability to ignore Obama's race in the debates?

Our ideas about candidates and about politics are shaped by what we see and hear on the Sunday morning talk shows, in the newspaper, on the local news, in political discussions with our friends. But I would also argue that our ideas about politics and about candidates are also shaped by other sources of information. By novels. By Web blogs. In this case, I believe that the production, circulation, and consumption of hip-hop looms large.

I grew up on rap and hip-hop. I remember *exactly* where I was the first time I heard "Rapper's Delight," the first rap single to get national airplay. The song was almost 15 minutes long, yet I memorized it. Hip-hop (which includes rap, but also DJing, graffiti, and break dancing) was like the air I breathed. For me, growing up in the 1980s, hip-hop was about young, urban, working-class black people (mostly males) speaking their truths to other young, urban, working-class black people. But now hip-hop has become much more than that, much more than a "black thing," coming not only to national but international prominence when some thought it a passing fad.

When Obama entered the race, most thought he would be unable to overcome white reluctance to vote for a black man.

Rap Music Is a Source of Information About Black Identity

Around the world MCs are rhyming in English, in German, in French, in Arabic, in Swahili, in Japanese, using the raw components of rap (two turntables and a microphone) to speak to their own conditions. At the inauguration, the Jumbotron showed scenes of the seated crowd, the VIPs. There were politicians, foreign dignitaries, movie directors (George Lucas, Steven Spielberg), and pop singers (Sting). But from where I was standing, the largest cheers went up for Shawn Carter (also known as JayZ) and Sean Combs (also known as Puff Daddy), two of rap's biggest figures.

Rap and hip-hop have long worked in black communities as sometimes crass and misogynistic entertainment but also as a source of information. Black youth consumers of rap music in the early 1990s were more likely to express support for the tenets of black nationalism than those not consuming rap. Similarly, black St. Louis youth who favored rap music were far more likely than other youth to be critical of the police. And my own research has found that black suburban youths exposed to hip-hop videos are far less likely to believe their neighborhoods are beset with the same problems that urban ones are. And this connection exists in part because rap music itself communicates information about urban space and about black identity. As hip-hop crossed over to the mainstream, not only did it give nonblacks a glimpse of a heavily stylized and fictionalized black urban space. It also connected whites with that experience.

Using a Hip-Hop Reference to Show Relevance

An example from the 2008 Democratic primary may be helpful here. Before the 2008 campaign began, most observers expected that Senator Hillary Clinton would become the Democrats' presidential candidate. She had already amassed a significant war chest, and she had the most name recognition of anyone among the likely candidates. When Obama entered the race, most thought he would be unable to overcome white reluctance to vote for a black man. After the Iowa caucus, it became clear that Obama was a legitimate candidate. Clinton had to change her tactics. One of her new critiques was that Obama was an elitist, out of touch. He was a candidate that the regular citizen (read: white, middle class) could not relate to. Obama would do well with minority and urban voters, but there was no way—so went the argument—that he would be able to speak to middle America. (The Republican Party and conservatives in general have used this critique over the last few elections with a great deal of success. George W. Bush, for example, was able to beat John Kerry in 2004 in part because Kerry had been successfully painted as being a member of the Northeastern blue-blooded elite.)

When Clinton used this line of attack against Obama, she gained a great deal of traction and cut into Obama's lead. Media pundits and political analysts thought that Obama's campaign would falter if he did not figure out how to respond. And Obama did. On April 17, the day after Clinton and Obama debated one another in North Carolina, Barack Obama held a packed town hall meeting in Raleigh, North Carolina. Talking about the media, and Clinton's propensity to paint her opponent as out of touch with regular Americans, Obama said the following:

"[The media] likes stirring up controversy . . . getting us to attack each other. And I've got to say, Senator Clinton looked in her element. She . . . was taking every opportunity to get a dig in there. . . . That's her right, to kind of twist the knife a little bit. Look, I understand that because that's the textbook Washington game. That's how our politics has . . . been played. That's the lesson she learned when the Republicans were doing the same thing to her back in the 1990s. So I understand it, and when you're running for the presidency you've got to expect it, and you've just gotta kinda let it—"

In 2008, one of the most popular singles was "Brush Your Shoulders Off" by JayZ.

And here Obama coolly brushed off one shoulder, then the other.

By placing Clinton's attack within a much broader critique of "politics as usual," Obama deftly categorized Clinton's comments as part of the very problem he was attempting to fight and replace. But in words, Obama criticized Clinton's practices without offering an alternative. Instead of articulating a response, Obama simply brushed his shoulders off. Yet when he performed this gesture, the crowd—which from video appears to have been racially mixed and age-diverse as well—went wild. They understood its meaning in the context of Obama's speech. More to the point, they at least appeared to have understood where Obama had gotten the gesture.

In 2008, one of the most popular singles was "Brush Your Shoulders Off" by JayZ:

> *If you feelin like a pimp, go on*
> *brush your*
>
> *shoulders*
>
> *off*
>
> *Ladies is pimps too, go on brush*
> *your shoulders*
>
> *off*
>
> *People are crazy baby, don't forget*
> *that boy told*
>
> *you*
>
> *Get, that, dirt off your shoulder*

In the song's video, every time the hook is played, JayZ can be seen brushing his shoulders off in the same manner as Obama. For JayZ, the song and the gesture were about taking the worst of what life presented and simply letting it roll off, not letting it move you away from your goals, from your mission. Obama could have tried in his speech to argue that he really *was* connected to "regular" Americans, that he *wasn't* an elitist. He could have noted that he was elected to the Senate by both urban *and* rural voters, that he supported causes that would help both Chicago and downstate Illinois. But this retort would likely have fallen on deaf ears, and given that Obama does not *look* like he could speak to rural communities, it would have fallen on blind eyes, too. Obama understood this. Instead of arguing that he was connected to real American constituencies, instead of arguing that he was in fact more attuned to the needs and wants of Americans than Clinton and the other candidates, he literally *performed* it.

Were we to boil the duties of elected officials down to one word, that word would be "represent."

Representing Hip Hop

After the speech, the Washington pundits weighed in. They were clueless almost to a man. They had no idea where Obama's gesture had come from. To them it was further proof of his elitism. Only later, after white and black bloggers chimed in, did they realize the source of the gesture. Here Obama secured *another* victory. Because they had no idea that Obama's gesture came from hip-hop, they, too, showed how out of touch they were. This further enhanced Obama's cachet. No other candidate could have pulled this off.

Were we to boil the duties of elected officials down to one word, that word would be "represent." "Representing" is a fundamental component of hip-hop as well. Rap MCs and breakdancing crews represent their neighborhoods and their cities, graffiti taggers represent themselves, all in an effort to express not just affinity but authenticity. Obama's gesture was a subtle signal to his constituency that he understood them and their issues. That he was authentic, legitimate. The gesture was quickly picked up by rap MCs, DJs, and graffiti artists. . . . Politically conscious rap MCs like Kanye West, Talbi Kweli, and Common have name-checked Obama in their raps. In the same way that national politicians routinely change their accent depending on where they are speaking. Obama used the gesture to indicate his connection with American communities. Not African-American communities—*American* communities. And although perhaps 10 years ago such a gesture might have been used only with (young) African-American audiences, with the explosion of hip-hop both nationally and globally, Obama could use such a gesture to speak to urban and rural America simultaneously.

Black President

Although African Americans turned out and voted for Obama in large numbers, they expressed two concerns about his campaign. Early on, understanding how his run would at least symbolically threaten America's racial regime, some were fearful that someone would assassinate Obama either during the campaign or after he was elected. Older African Americans with direct experience with Jim Crow-era racism were particularly affected here. After blacks realized that he had a real shot at victory, some wondered whether he would really support "black" interests. Although the question of whether Obama was really "black" was a non-starter in black communities—seeing his (black) wife and children quickly put to rest those claims—some did wonder whether Obama would be invested in dealing with the issues of poverty and discrimination that concern many African Americans, particularly during the current economic crisis.

One of the most interesting attempts to wrestle with these concerns was a hip-hop song, Nas' "Black President":

What's the black pres. thinkin' on
election night?

Is it how can I protect my life?

Protect my wife?

Protect my rights?

... KKK is like "what the f---,"
loadin' they guns

up

Loadin' mine too, ready to ride

Cause I'm ridin' with my crew

He dies—we die too

But on a positive side,

I think Obama provides hope—and
challenges

minds

Of all races and colors to erase
the hate

And try and love one another, so
many political snakes

We in need of a break

I'm thinkin' I can trust this brotha

But will he keep it way real?

Every innocent nigga in jail—gets
out on appeal

When he wins—will he really
care still?

Nas wonders aloud whether Obama himself is thinking about the possibility he may be assassinated. He fuses Obama's thoughts about protecting his own life (and that of his family) with Nas' thoughts about his own rights. I referred to Obama's authenticity above. As an MC, Nas takes his concern with authenticity ("will he keep it way real?") and goes beyond the symbolic by wondering whether Obama will truly represent the political interests of African Americans, defined here as being interested in dealing with the horrific effects of the prison-industrial complex. Rap was used not only by Obama to establish and cement his political stance as, on the one hand, an outsider (compared to other Washington, D.C., politicians), and on the other a political intimate (of urban, suburban, and rural constituencies). It was, and still is, used by people outside of traditional politics to speak to his potential.

All This from Hip Hop

In 2004, Sean Combs held a "White Party"—all guests were required to wear white from head to toe—at his estate in the Hamptons. At the party he toted an actual copy of the Declaration of Independence that he borrowed from television producer Norman Lear. He used the event (and the borrowed copy of the Declaration) to announce the formation of a *political* group "Citizen Change." His goal was to use rap to organize young voters. I don't think that Combs had any clue that just four years later he would see a black man sworn in as president. And I don't think that 40 years ago, when black and Puerto Rican youth created what we now know as hip-hop, they thought someday it would span the globe and be used as a tool of empowerment, resistance, and political accommodation. But thinking back on Obama's campaign, on his election, and on contemporary black and American politics, all I can think of is this snippet from Lauryn Hill's speech, given several years ago when she was awarded a Grammy for the groundbreaking *The Miseducation of Lauryn Hill*: "All this, from hip-hop."

Hip-Hop Gives Youths a Needed Outlet for Self-Expression

Carolee Walker

Carolee Walker is a staff writer for Info USA, a public informa-tion website published by the US Department of State.

African-American and Latino teens with turntables and time on their hands in the 1970s invented hip-hop—a musical style born in the United States and now the center of a huge music and fashion industry around the world.

Hip-hop began 30 years ago in the Bronx, a borough of New York City and a neighborhood that seemed to exemplify the bleakness of poor urban places.

Using turntables to spin old, worn records, kids in the South Bronx began to talk over music, creating an entirely new music genre and dance form. This "talking over," or MC-ing (rapping) and DJing (audio mixing and scratching), be-came the essence of rap music, break dance and graffiti art, according to Marvette Perez, curator at the Smithsonian Institution's National Museum of American History in Wash-ington, which launched its collecting initiative "Hip-Hop Won't Stop: The Beat, The Rhymes, The Life" in 2006.

"Out of this forgotten, bleak place, an incredible tradition was born," Perez said.

"It's important for young people to know that their stories matter," said Jade Foster, an English and humanities teacher at Ballou Senior High School in Washington, which hosted a summer program in 2009 encouraging students to express

Carolee Walker, "Hip-Hop Music an Outlet for Self-Expression," InfoUSA (http://infousa.state.gov), Bureau of International Information Programs (IIP), U.S. Depart-ment of State, Sept. 23, 2009.

themselves through hip-hop. "It's important for young people to know that their stories are relevant to their lives and their histories."

> *Hip-hop [can be traced] from its origins in the late 1970s ... to its status today as a multibillion-dollar industry.*

From the beginning, style has been a big element of hip-hop, Perez said. "Hip-hop tells the story of music, but also of urban America and its style."

"With the significant contributions from the hip-hop community, we will be able to place hip-hop in the continuum of American history and present a comprehensive exhibition," Brent D. Glass, director of the museum, said.

The museum's multiyear project traces hip-hop from its origins in the late 1970s, as an expression of urban black and Latino youth culture, to its status today as a multibillion-dollar industry worldwide. Perez said they have received collections from hip-hop artists including Grandmaster Flash, Afrika Bambaataa, Kool Herc, Ice T, Fab 5 Freddy, Crazy Legs and MC Lyte.

An Important Cultural Contribution

"Hip-hop is the most important contribution to the American cultural landscape since blues and jazz," said hip-hop artist and promoter, filmmaker and producer Fab 5 Freddy, born Fred Brathwaite. "It is dominant in every youth culture in every country." According to statistics gathered in 2009 by Russell Simmons and Accel Partners, today's global hip-hop community comprises 24 million people between the ages of 19 and 34, including a range of nationalities, ethnic groups and religions.

"One thing that is applicable to every generation of teenagers is urgency," music producer and film director Mark

Shimmel said. Everything about hip-hop—the sound, the lyrics, the style, the language—conveys that sense of urgency.

"The sociological and cultural impact of rock 'n' roll pales in comparison to what hip-hop has been able to accomplish," Shimmel said. "Hip-hop is the singular most important melding of black and white cultures that has ever existed in the United States."

Urban music, like Motown, "worked for white audiences," he said, "but you did not see blacks and whites together at live concerts."

Finding Similarities in the Differences

"Hip-hop changed that because it was about fashion and language from the beginning, and—most importantly—captured a sense of urgency that teenagers in the suburbs and in the cities could relate to," he said. "When hip-hop artists wrote about the world they saw in the inner city, black and white teens recognized that the isolation of suburbia was not much different."

Fab 5 Freddy, host of the television show Yo! MTV Raps in the 1980s, said hip-hop is successful because the music is "infectious" and because it allows people to express themselves in a positive, dynamic and consciousness-raising way. "Hip-hop is for everybody with an open ear," he said.

In 1985, when Run-D.M.C.'s King of Rock became the first hip-hop record to "go platinum," an award given by the Recording Industry Association of America for the sale of 1 million records, it was apparent that hip-hop had crossed over from African-American and Latino urban music into white culture, Shimmel said. In 2005, OutKast's Grammy Award for Album of the Year was a first for a hip-hop album.

Shimmel said hip-hop today has not strayed far from its South Bronx roots. "Every musical form evolves," Shimmel said. "Hip-hop started in New York, and it was interpreted differently in Los Angeles, and then the South added another element. It has evolved, but it hasn't changed."

Today hip-hop music, poetry and art prepare teens for every avenue in life, teacher Foster said. Hip-hop helps develop speech and build confidence, she said.

Looking Past Antisocial Elements to Global Impact

Perez said some hip-hop music is notable for its disrespect of women, and the museum does not plan to dismiss this aspect of hip-hop. The so-called "gangsta" rap in the 1990s, with lyrics promoting drug use, violence and tagging, a form of graffiti used to mark gang territories, is a component of the hip-hop culture that cannot be ignored, Perez said, but "on the whole, the majority of hip-hop is creative and positive."

Hip-hop's influence both musically and culturally is global, Perez said. "The technique resonates throughout the United States and the world."

CHAPTER 3

Is Rap Music Harmful to Women?

Overview: Rap Lyrics Face Scrutiny

Brian Garrity

Brian Garrity is a senior business writer at Billboard *magazine.*

Maybe this sounds familiar: Hip-hop, coming off a year of declining sales and bemoaning a lack of new superstar talent, sees its problems further mount as a firestorm of media controversy swirls around its lyrical content and video imagery.

Major label groups are accused of profiteering from racial, sexual and socio-economic exploitation. With a variety of watchdog organizations on the attack and fears of legislative intervention looming, the recording industry attempts to police hip-hop content in an effort to find the "delicate balance between artists' rights to express themselves and the legitimate concerns of parents and corporate responsibility." Complaints by artists of the potential for a chilling effect on creativity follow.

Only the year isn't 2007—it's 1995. And Warner Music Group (WMG)—which had already been taking heat for years for so-called "gangsta rap" releases by Tupac Shakur and Snoop Dogg, and hardcore releases like Ice-T's Body Count via its Interscope/Death Row-unit—sees the issue come to a head in the media with a pending release from Snoop crew members Tha Dogg Pound.

As the current public debate over racially charged and sexist content in hip-hop rages, it is important to remember that controversies in a genre that specializes in controversy are cyclical and to be expected. But should media scrutiny of the issue intensify, it is also noteworthy that such situations can also have serious implications for the power dynamics in the music business, depending on how companies react to public pressure.

Labels often release "clean" and "explicit" versions of hip-hop and rap albums.

In the last major go-around on hip-hop content, now more than a decade old (though certainly there have been numerous other smaller controversies since), the issue wouldn't go away until WMG parent Time Warner made the fateful decision to rid itself of its 50% stake in Interscope Records—a move that has haunted WMG ever since.

What it will take to quiet the current dispute remains to be seen. In a bid to mute the genre's current critics, the Hip-Hop Summit Action Network (HSAN), a group led by Def Jam Records co-founder Russell Simmons and NAACP head Benjamin Chavis, is recommending that the recording industry and broadcasters voluntarily bleep and/or delete the words ["b**ch"], "ho" and the "n word" from songs. The recommendation follows a widely reported meeting of the leaders of the hip-hop community in the wake of the Don Imus controversy.

Of course, radio and MTV already police such content to a large extent, and labels often release "clean" and "explicit" versions of hip-hop and rap albums.

But HSAN CEO Chavis says more can be done. He argues that there is no consistency or standard used in editing clean versions of records.

"It's not banning," Chavis says. "It is deleting, bleeping and removing those from clean versions, which the music industry is supposed to do anyway."

The Rev. Al Sharpton, for his part, has pledged to buy stock in companies that release and broadcast hip-hop, in order to put additional pressure on the industry to better police lyrical content.

That approach has precedents as well. In 1995, C. Delores Tucker, chairman of the National Political Congress of Black Women, helped ante pressure on Time Warner and WMG by attending a shareholders meeting and denouncing the company's support of hip-hop.

Rosen warns that hip-hop remains an easy target for politicians and culture critics.

The current flap over hip-hop comes at a sensitive time for publicly traded companies like WMG, which has made building its urban music efforts a priority under the leadership of CEO Edgar Bronfman Jr. and U.S. recorded music CEO Lyor Cohen, and is attempting to pursue a merger with EMI. Should the scandal intensify and spook investors, that could cause a dip in the company's already fragile stock price, which in turn could cause problems for its consolidation strategy, analysts say.

But Hilary Rosen, former chairman/CEO of the RIAA and now an industry consultant, says there is a key difference between earlier hip-hip content controversies she helped guide the music business through and the current one: In the current crisis there is no one record company or artist that has emerged as a focal point of criticism.

Still, Rosen warns that hip-hop remains an easy target for politicians and culture critics and that its ability to avoid the threat of regulation and further media criticism will hinge on its ability to lead the conversation by asking hard questions about itself.

So far labels are yet to announce support for HSAN's recommendations or suggest other measures. And no further meetings involving label heads have been scheduled.

"Those who want to batten down the hatches and wait for this to blow over can achieve that. Because it will," Rosen says.

"But those who want to see new progressive values move into this area will view this as an opportunity."

Rap Music Objectifies, Degrades, and Exploits Black Women

Tracy Sharpley-Whiting

Tracy Sharpley-Whiting is the director of African American and Diaspora Studies and a professor at Vanderbilt University.

Today, demeaning, degrading and objectifying Black women are undeniably profitable pastimes. From the cross-dressing male 'Mammy' à la comedian Eddie Murphy's recent turn in the $50 million-dollar-generating Hollywood vehicle *Norbit* to Don Imus's "nappy-headed hos" kerfuffle to Rush Limbaugh's referring to the accuser in the Duke lacrosse rape case as a "ho" to the "we don't love them hos" ethos of much of commercial hip hop, a culture of disrespect, with Black women on the receiving end, packaged as entertainment, permeates American popular culture.

There are iPod commercials that allude to strip club culture featuring an abundantly rumped Black woman holding onto a pole on a public bus. And then there is the Quentin Tarantino ode to alpha females in the second film of the double feature *Grindhouse* where the lone Black female character is the only one to utter ad nauseam an expletive that describes a female dog. Indeed, such antics have risen to the level of art, whereby entertainers believe they should receive a "free pass" because they are merely performing their craft— whether it be crude, curmudgeonly shock jocks, or grill-wearing, pimped out rap artists.

Tracy Sharpley-Whiting, Testimony before the House Subcommittee on Commerce, Trade and Consumer Protection, Subcommittee on Commerce, Trade and Consumer Protection, "From Imus to Industry: The Business of Stereotypes and Degrading Images," House Committee on Energy and Commerce, United States House of Representatives, September 25, 2007.

The Historical Roots of Disrespect

Although most Americans associate this culture of disrespect with hip hop culture, ironically such characterizations find their roots in our nation's beginnings. In 1781, a mere five years after penning that hallowed document of a new nation, *The Declaration of Independence*, which prized freedom while sanctioning perpetual bondage, our founding father Thomas Jefferson set his sights on writing on his beloved state of Virginia. In between pages on flora and fauna in *Notes on the State of Virginia*, Jefferson delivered a prophecy about race-based slavery in the United States. Of slavery, he would write, "it was a great political and moral evil," and that he "trembled for my country when I reflect that God is just, that His justice cannot sleep forever. . . . Deep rooted prejudices entertained by whites; ten thousand recollections, by the blacks, of the injuries they have sustained . . . will divide us into parties . . . end[ing] in the extermination of the one or the other races." Of Blacks in general, he concluded that "whether originally a distinct race, or made distinct by time and circumstances [they] are inferior to the whites in the endowments both of body and mind." And of Black women, he suggested that they were more "ardent" and preferred "uniformly" by the male "Oranootan" over females of "his own species." There were no orangutans to be found in Virginia to substantiate such an observation. This fact was of little consequence to Thomas Jefferson.

Jefferson's paradox has had an enduring legacy in the United States.

A deeply complicated and conflicted man, Jefferson, as is widely acknowledged, had a prolonged intimate relationship with the young slave girl Sally Hemmings. With *Notes on the State of Virginia*, our nation's third president sealed an odious racial-sexual contract within our national fabric regarding

Black women. Jefferson's paradox has had an enduring legacy in the United States. Against this unequivocal founding doctrine, Black women have been continuously struggling both in the courts of law and public opinion, in our very own communities, and as of late, on America's airwaves.

Black Women Defend Themselves

From slave narratives like Harriet Jacob's *Incidents in the Life of a Slave Girl* to post-emancipation writings such as Anna Julia Cooper's *A Voice from the South, by A Woman from the South*, Black women have been steadfast in decrying attacks on their character and morality. When after the president of the Missouri Press Association wrote an open letter addressed to an Englishwoman attempting to cast aspersions on the credibility of anti-lynching crusader Ida B. Wells, he made plain that Black women "had no sense of virtue" and "character." In response, the black women's club movement organized in July 1895 to defend their name.

Hip hop culture is certainly waist deep in the muck of this race-gender chauvinism.

Despite our strides in every area of American life—nearly two million college-educated Black women out-earning their white and Latina counterparts; one in four of us occupies managerial or professional positions,—the profits to be had at our expense are far greater than the costs of caricaturing our personhood.

Looking in the Mirror

Our own complicity in our objectification requires some scrutiny as well. Consumer culture seduces many of us into selling ourselves short in the marketplace of ideas and desire. The range of our successes and the diversity of our lives and career paths have been congealed in the mainstream media into video vixens thanks to Karrine Steffans' bestselling *Confessions of a Video Vixen* or shake dancers given the frenzy surrounding the Duke rape case and hip hop culture's collaboration with the multi-billion dollar adult entertainment industry.

That sexism and misogyny appear to be working overtime in America to box us into these very narrow depictions of Black womanhood are part and parcel of the Jeffersonian contract. Hip hop culture is certainly waist deep in the muck of this race-gender chauvinism. Male feelings of displacement in a perceived topsy-turvy female-dominated world, increased competition from women and girls in every facet of American life contribute to Black-male-on-Black-female-gender drive bys. And Black women's seeming resiliency, despite America's continuing race and gender biases, our strengths, are flung back at us and condensed into clichés such as the late New York Senator Daniel Patrick Moynihan's "emasculating superwomen," or better still—that "b-word."

Though America drinks to the bursting from that Jeffersonian well, it is imperative that women become more politically and socially conscious about the choices we make and the opportunities we take. As a writer and scholar and member of the so-called "hip hop generation," I find aspects of American popular culture with its global reach and entrepreneurial and innovative spirit deeply gratifying and simultaneously painfully disturbing. For it has become abundantly clear that it is not so much that we women don't count. We do—in obviously various insidious ways. But we also don't add up to much—certainly not more than the profits, in the billions, to be had at our expense.

Take the Debate Over Degrading Rap Videos Off Mute

Michele Goodwin

Michele Goodwin is the Everett Fraser Professor in Law at the University of Minnesota. Her work has appeared in such publications as the Chronicle of Higher Education, The New York Times, *and the* Christian Science Monitor.

My daughter is 11 years old. Like other girls her age, she enjoys text messaging, going to movies, and she wants braces. She also happens to be a straight A student, winner of her school's science fair, and an accomplished classical dancer at a premier ballet school in Chicago. She is also African-American. Despite her accomplishments and what some might say is a "good start," I am a helicopter parent (I hover constantly).

Because the horrible images portrayed of black girls and women as gyrating, hypersexual, insolent, irresponsible, and utterly available prey may stigmatize her and could lead to violence against her, I worry. Naively, I assumed this could be managed by monitoring the MTV, VH1, and, worst of all, BET [Black Entertainment Television] channels in our home. Yet, I shouldn't have been surprised when my daughter's new classmate from the Philippines, unprovoked, called my daughter a "stupid ho" and "b-ch," terms of endearment used by some black men in videos and rap music. When confronted by the principal, the boy admitted addressing my daughter that way, but argued in his defense that he learned it from black men on TV.

A controversy [in the summer of 2006] involving Troi To-rian (aka DJ Star), a popular New York disc jockey, and his spate of on-air sexual and violent threats against a little girl illustrates the perverse state of affairs. To taunt a rival disc jockey, DJ Star asked callers to reveal the whereabouts of Rashawn Casey's 4-year-old daughter. He made highly descriptive, on-air references to possible sexual interactions with her. He offered a $500 reward for any information about where the little girl attends school.

Nothing could be further from the truth than the notion that accountability, integrity, and self-growth are "destructive" to black Americans.

Dirty Little Secrets

This kind of lewd public commentary demonstrates a certain kind of 21st-century minstrelsy and reveals a complex state of intraracial affairs. Within the African-American community, issues of sexual violence, including rape, incest, and abuse are typically closeted. Black people seem to fear that if whites were to get wind of such problems it might exacerbate racism and perpetuate stereotypes.

For example, Michael Eric Dyson, winner of the 2006 NAACP [National Association for the Advancement of Colored People] Image Award, has publicly criticized Bill Cosby for exposing dirty little secrets such as drug use, parental neglect, and other issues in the black community. Professor Dyson describes Mr. Cosby as being insensitive and pushing a "destructive" agenda. Dyson claims Cosby won't admit that racism exists. Nothing could be further from the truth than the notion that accountability, integrity, and self-growth are "destructive" to black Americans. Neither are these right-wing, Republican, or "white" values.

Moreover, we are only deluding ourselves to think no one notices this terrible self-destruction. After all, BET is quite public, as are videos on MTV and the criminal records of those caught in the matrix of celebrity and "gangsta" life. Ironically, it remains black men who primarily portray black women as hypersexual. From once exporting images of respected if not noble civil rights leaders and activists, the black image now includes desperate sexual depravity. Most important, I wonder why these conversations must happen in the race closet when the videos and behavior are very public, unapologetic, and ubiquitous.

Hip-Hop Feminism Can Change the Hip-Hop Community and Society

Akoto Ofori-Atta

Akoto Ofori-Atta is the assistant editor of The Root, a daily on-line news source devoted to news and commentary from the African American perspective.

Joan Morgan coined the phrase back in 1999, but what does hip-hop feminism look like today? Is it Queen Latifah? Nicki Minaj? Or the 10-year-old girl calling out Lil Wayne?

In 1992 Dr. Dre released his single "Bitches Ain't Sh--," complete with a chorus that emphatically reduces women to nothing but "hoes and tricks." In 1996 Akinyele famously sang "Put It In Your Mouth," a song that flooded radio airwaves and clubs across the country.

Fast-forward to 2003, and Nelly releases a video for his single "Tip Drill," in which he famously slides a credit card between the cheeks of a video vixen's bottom. And then there was, of course, the Don Imus incident, when he justified his "nappy-headed ho" comment by arguing that black men regularly call their women out of their names in hip-hop songs.

There is no shortage of these cringe-inducing moments that have made women question their relationship to hip-hop. But these moments don't go completely uncontested. From Queen Latifah's "U.N.I.T.Y." ("Who you callin' a bitch?") to a 10-year-old's heartfelt plea to Lil Wayne urging him to speak highly of women, hip-hop feminism has almost always been just as audible as the crass catcalls. While one might be hard-pressed to find a song of the "Put It In Your Mouth" variety in heavy rotation today, hip-hop feminists still have a job to do in railing against a male-dominated culture.

How do women actively participate in a culture that seems to hate them so vehemently?

Hip-hop feminists are like other feminists in that they advocate for gender equality. Where they part ways from other feminist groups is that they operate in and identify as part of hip-hop culture, as expressed in their choices in music, dance, art and politics.

Leaving Behind Rap's Misogyny

For some, the term "hip-hop feminism" offers up quite the enigma. Critics position misogyny as hip-hop's cardinal sin, which raises the obvious question: How do women actively participate in a culture that seems to hate them so vehemently? For self-described hip-hop feminists, attempting to answer that question is not their only task, since understanding what hip-hop feminism is and isn't goes far beyond responding to women-bashing sentiment.

"I could care less about what these boys are expressing in their lyrics, whether it's misogynistic or sexist or not, because we've had that conversation," says Joan Morgan, author of the seminal book *When Chickenheads Come Home to Roost: My Life as a Hip-Hop Feminist*. Today's hip-hop feminists, she says, should be focused on addressing other critical issues, like challenging the "respectability politics" that keep black women from freely expressing their sexuality.

Morgan did not coin the term "hip-hop feminist" until 1999, but rap's pro-woman consciousness dates back further, with artists like Queen Latifah, MC Lyte, Tupac and Eve making music with a distinctly feminist sensibility. But promoting and recognizing artists and lyrics that support women in hip-hop is only part of hip-hop feminism's agenda.

"I was never talking about tracks made by female artists," Morgan says of her book, which was the first to articulate the dichotomy of hip-hop feminism. "I was talking about hip-hop culture, and the ways that people move through it. I don't think a hip-hop feminist critique can do the work it needs to do if it can't analyze all of it."

Black Feminism vs. Hip-Hop Feminism

To be certain, hip-hop feminism was born out of a need to understand the many cultural, social and political conditions that afflicted women of what Baraki Kitwana called the hip-hop generation, comprised of people born between 1965 and 1985. Black feminism, a wave of thought and activism largely influenced by the civil rights and black power movements, was not equipped to consider the issues of women belonging to the hip-hop generation.

Although hip-hop feminism has gone through phases, it has always, at some level, dealt with . . . incongruities.

Hip-hop's babies weren't dealing directly with issues of invisibility brought on by systems of segregation the way the generations were that came before them. Instead, they were grappling with being front and center as the most loved and most hated stars of global popular culture. The popularity of hip-hop made black youth cool and desirable, which was in complete opposition to the unavoidable stereotypes in the media that illustrated them as gang members, welfare queens, drug dealers and teen mothers.

"The manifestos of black feminism, while they helped me to understand the importance of articulating language to combat oppression, didn't give me the language to explore things that were not black and white, but things that were in the gray," Morgan says. "And that gray is very much represented in hip-hop."

This gray area includes the contradictions of loving an art that is reluctant to include you; loving men who, at times, refuse to portray you in your totality; and rejecting sexual objectification while actively and proudly embracing your sexuality. Although hip-hop feminism has gone through phases, it has always, at some level, dealt with these incongruities.

"Hip-hop feminists have been consistent in championing women's rights, which encompasses everything from sexuality to abuse," says Marcyliena Morgan, founding director of the Hip-Hop Archive in the W.E.B. Du Bois Institute at Harvard University. "And that has always been irrespective of what men in hip-hop were doing."

What the Future Holds

So what should hip-hop feminism look like in 2011? Instead of being reduced to an anti-misogyny movement or to a rallying cry to give more female MCs the mic, hip-hop feminists hope that it will incorporate a women-centric worldview, where the realities of the hip-hop generation's women are taken into consideration at every turn. It doesn't just complain about the lack of female MCs but actively addresses the reasons there are fewer female MCs now than there were in the late 1980s, and why there are only a few types of female MCs that make it to hip-hop notoriety.

Joan Morgan also thinks that hip-hop feminism needs to evolve so that it can address the curious case of hip-hop's most current and colorful female character, Nicki Minaj. Minaj may be the most visible example of female resistance from an artist. Whether she is professing, as she did on Kanye West's song "Monster," "You could be the king, but watch the queen conquer," or being open about her bi-curiosity, Minaj embraces female power and challenges norms of sexuality that black female hip-hop artists have not always embraced.

"We don't even know what to make of her, and we don't even know if she's straight or not," Morgan says. "I want to see the creation of language that pushes us to have a more indepth conversation about Nikki Minaj, that doesn't just compare her to Lil' Kim, because she is not Lil' Kim."

Forging a Hip-Hop Identity

And perhaps Minaj doesn't know what to make of herself. As she once told an interviewer, "[W]hen I grew up I saw females doing certain things, and I thought I had to do that exactly. The female rappers of my day spoke about sex a lot . . . and I thought that to have the success they got, I would have to represent the same thing, when in fact I didn't have to represent the same thing."

Hip-hop feminism, just like any branch of feminism, should use activism to effect real social change.

For up-and-coming female MCs, the opportunity to be recognized as Grade A performers who can co-exist and share stages with Grade A male rappers may be the difference between a hip-hop feminism that works and one that doesn't. Nicki Lynette, a Chicago-based artist whose music blends hip-hop, funk and pop, says that she didn't realize she held feminist views until she was asked to do an all-female showcase and mixtape.

"I said no because I think it's anti-feminist to make women in hip-hop a sideshow," Lynette told *The Root*. "A show that includes several hot MCs, both male and female, and is less concerned about making the distinction between men and women makes more sense to me."

But perhaps hip-hop feminism's most important task is staying keenly attuned to the needs of the hip-hop community. Hip-hop feminism, just like any branch of feminism, should use activism to effect real social change. This requires all members of the hip-hop generation to get on board.

So it's not just women who are tasked with tapping into the creative resources that give hip-hop's women a voice. "Mark Anthony Neal's work is a good example of this," says Marcyliena Morgan. "The one thing that hip-hop feminism has taught anyone is that feminism must include the efforts of the entire community, men and women alike."

The Hip-Hop Community Works to Address Misogyny Issues

Davey D

Journalist and hip-hop activist Davey D is the cohost of Hard Knock Radio, *a nationally syndicated daily radio program that focuses on hip-hop and politics. He is also a columnist for the* San Jose Mercury News *and teaches at San Francisco State University.*

Last night (March 14, 2012) the Oakland [California] chapter of 100 Black Men and Safe Passages, an organization from 'Tha Town' that is in the forefront of dealing with domestic violence and sexual assault, hooked up with members of the Hip Hop community to hold a town hall meeting inside City Hall. The topic was misogyny, teen violence and the influence Rap Music has on our behavior.

Lemme just say this from jump street, what took place last night was riveting, honest, powerful and inspiring. It wasn't a gripe session or a finger-pointing rap bashing occasion. It wasn't an event where two generations (Hip Hop and Civil Rights) found themselves at odds blaming one another.

What you had at the Oakland town hall was a community who clearly understands there are important issues at hand impacting young minds and we have to go in another direction.

One of the highlights of the town hall was the discussion with Bay Area rap pioneer Too Short. But folks were clear from the beginning these issues are systemic and go way beyond one rapper, one magazine or one incident. However, the recent controversy around Too Short giving explicit "fatherly advice" to middle school age boys in an online video hosted by rap publication *XXL* had put him on the hot seat.

Some of the most powerful statements came from the young survivors of rape and sexual assault.

Short said he takes full responsibility for his actions and wanted to be part of the conversation to help rectify and repair the damage and disappointment he caused. Many felt he was candid and forthcoming with his remarks and the evening ended with him noting this is just a starting point and him appealing to other artists in the room to change direction, expand their horizons and re-define the legacy of Oakland rap.

Survivors and Statistics

Last night's town hall saw, in addition to Too Short, other key stake holders including elected officials, community activists and local artists come together with a spirit of love, a desire to heal and eager to find ways to bring about brighter tomorrows. Some of the most powerful statements came from the young survivors of rape and sexual assault who shared their perspectives and solutions.

During the town hall, Alameda County supervisor Keith Carson along with a couple of members of 100 Black Men set the tone, by discussing the harrowing statistics around sexual assault. Carson noted that every couple of minutes a woman is sexually assaulted. He said over 10 million kids had witnessed domestic violence and one out of 5 teenage girls has been assaulted. He also pointed out that since 2005 over 2 million boys/men have been sexually assaulted.

Carson surmised that the figures are probably much higher. He was just noting what had been reported. He also pointed out that rather than we point fingers and play the blame game, we come at this from the spirit of sparking dialogue with a goal of getting solutions to turn the tide.

Dereca Blackmon, who is part of the We Are the 44% Coalition, gave a great presentation on the commodification of songs celebrating sexual abuse and degenerate behavior. She noted that many have come to confuse videos with real life. She broke down how that impacts us all.

Afterwards Blackmon sat down with Too Short and had a 20 minute revealing discussion about the music industry, the role artists should take in turning things around and his own personal journey to understanding some of the issues being addressed. He talked about the *XXL* controversy and the eye-opening conversation he had with writer Dream Hampton.

The evening concluded with a panel discussion where we heard some power statements and solutions from young activists and artists, some of whom are survivors of rape, sexual assault and violence.

The mood at the end of the evening was upbeat with many feeling very inspired. Sadly and in typical fashion some of that good energy was dampened by what was shown on the evening news. . . .

We can . . . cit[e] examples where the activities of artists . . . have led to town hall-style meetings . . . and TV debates.

A Time for Self-Reflection

What took place last night [March 13, 2012] was by no means new or unique in terms of the topics discussed. Every couple of years something pops off and captures the attention of the media or activists and hence such discussions unfold. A few years ago we saw this topic broached after radio host Don Imus went on air [and] called women on a college basketball team, "Nappy Headed Hos". His remarks set off a firestorm with people calling for Imus to be fired. He in turn countered and claimed that he made the unsavory remarks because he was influenced by rap music. That in turn led to many of us having reflective self-examination type discussions.

A couple of years prior to Imus's remarks, we had a situation involving rap star Nelly, who was shown on a video to his popular song "Tip Drill" swiping a credit card thru the cheeks of a bikini clad dancer. Again it set off a storm of controversy leading up to Spelman College rejecting him when he was scheduled to come on campus and do a bone marrow benefit and bring awareness to the plight of his cancer stricken sister.

We can go on and on citing examples where the activities of artists ranging from 2 Live Crew to NWA to 2Pac to Snoop Dogg to Jay-Z and 50 Cent have led to town hall-style meetings, vigorous radio and TV debates, and Senate and Congressional Hearings.

As was mentioned earlier, last night's Town Hall, which was held in the chambers of the Oakland City Council, came in the wake of [an] incident last month involving Bay Area rap pioneer Too Short and *XXL Magazine*. The magazine produced an online video that depicted Too Short dispensing "fatherly advice" to young 12 & 13-year-old boys on how to "turn out young girls" and "take it to the hole."

We Are the 44 Percent Coalition

This outraged a number of Hip Hop generation Black and Latina activists, writers and scholars like Joan Morgan, Rosa Clemente and Dream Hampton to name a few, who felt that not only did this cross some major fault lines but [it] was the nail in the coffin for what they saw as increasing attacks on young girls, women of color and women in general.

These aforementioned sisters linked up with other women and a growing number of male allies like Dr. Marc Anthony

Neal, Lumumba Akinwole-Bandele and filmmaker Byron Hurt, to name a few, who also shared in the outrage to form the We Are the 44% Coalition.

We Are the 44% Coalition felt it was important that awareness be raised around the fact that 44% of sexual assault and rape survivors are under the age of 18 and that as a group they push to create a climate where what Too Short & *XXL* did is never repeated by other artists and publications.

A Push for Solutions

They demanded that Harris Publication, which owns *XXL*, take steps to fire the editor (Vanessa Satten) and donate space in the magazine to have issues of sexual assault adequately addressed.

They "blew the whistle" on Too Short and demanded he educate himself and start working with organizations in our community that deal with sexual assault.

Soon after forming, weekly online twitter chats started taking place with the hash tag #ItsBiggerThan2Short. It is there that many started [to] come together to discuss these issues, demands and craft solutions.

During last night's town hall there was a call to action for all of us to not allow the daily assaults on women both verbal and physical [to] become normalized. Many recognize there is currently an all-out war on women both within our community and the society at large that is systemic and far-reaching.

CHAPTER 4

Does Rap Music Perpetuate Violence?

Overview: The Complex Debate About Violence and Rap

Tricia Rose

Tricia Rose is a pioneering voice in the field of hip-hop scholarship. In addition to The Hip Hop Wars, *from which this viewpoint is drawn, she is the author of* Black Noise: Rap Music and Black Culture in Contemporary America, *as well as numerous magazine and journal articles about hip-hop. She is a professor of Africana Studies at Brown University.*

A key aspect of much of the criticism that has been leveled at hip hop is the claim that it glorifies, encourages, and thus causes violence. This argument goes as far back as the middle to late 1980s—the so-called golden age of hip hop—when politically radical hip hop artists, such as Public Enemy, who referred to direct and sometimes armed resistance against racism "by any means necessary," were considered advocates of violence. It is important to zero in on the specific issue of violence because this was the most highly visible criticism of hip hop for over a decade. The concern over hip hop and violence peaked in the early to mid-1990s when groups like N.W.A. from Los Angeles found significant commercial success through a gang-oriented repertoire of stories related especially to anti-police sentiment. N.W.A.'s 1989 song "F--- the Police"—with lyrics boasting that when they are done, "it's gonna be a bloodbath of cops dyin' in LA"—was at the epicenter of growing fears that rappers' tales of aggression and frustration (which many critics mistakenly perceived as simply pro-criminal statements of intent) were stirring up violent behavior among young listeners. The 1992 debut commercial single for Snoop Doggy Dogg, "Deep Cover" (from the film of the same name), garnered attention because of Snoop's laconic rap style, Dr. Dre's extra-funky beats, and the chorus phrase "187 on a undercover cop" ("187" is the police code for homicide). As what we now call gangsta rap began to move to the commercial center stage, the worry that increasing portrayals of violence in rap lyrics might encourage fans to imitate them evolved into a belief that the rappers were *themselves* criminals—representing their own violent acts in the form of rhyme. Snoop's own criminal problems authenticated his lyrics and added to the alarm about gangsta rap. As this shift in commercial hip hop has solidified, many vocal public critics have begun to characterize violence-portraying lyrics as autobiographical thuggery to a soundtrack. In turn, this link of violent lyrics in hip hop and behavior has been used in the legal arena by both defense and prosecuting attorneys. . . . Hip hop lyrics have indeed been considered strong influences. Increasingly, this connection has been extended into the realm of establishing character in murder trials. Prosecutors around the country have buttressed their cases with defendants' penned lyrics as evidence of their criminal-mindedness.

Causality Should Be Questioned

The criticism that hip hop advocates and thus causes violence relies on the unsubstantiated but widely held belief that listening to violent stories or consuming violent images *directly* encourages violent behavior. This concern was raised vis-à-vis violent video games during the 1980s, but also more recently, in relation to heavy metal music. Although the direct link between consumption and action may appear to be commonsensical, studies have been unable to provide evidence that confirms it. Recent challenges to the video game industry's sale of exceptionally gory and violent video games were stymied by the absence of such data and confirmation. Direct behavioral effect is, of course, a difficult thing to prove in scientific terms, since many recent and past factors—both individual and social—can contribute to a person's actions at any given time. The absence of direct proof doesn't mean that such imagery and lyrics are without negative impact. I am not arguing *for* the regular consumption of highly violent images and stories, nor am I saying that what we consume has no impact on us. Clearly, everything around us, past and present, has an impact on us, to one degree or another. Studies do show that violent music lyrics have been documented as increasing aggressive thoughts and feelings. High-saturation levels of violent imagery and action (in our simulated wars and fights in sports, film, music, and television but also, more significantly, in our real wars in the Middle East) clearly do not support patient, peaceful, cooperative actions and responses in our everyday lives.

We live in a popular cultural world in which violent stories, images, lyrics, and performances occupy a wide cross-section of genres and mediums.

However, the argument for one-to-one causal linking among storytelling, consumption, and individual action should be questioned, given the limited evidence to support this claim. And, even more important, the blatantly selective application of worries about violence in some aspects of popular culture and everyday life should be challenged for its targeting of individuals and groups who are already overly and problematically associated with violence. So, what may appear to be genuine concern over violence in entertainment winds up stigmatizing some expressions (rap music) and the groups with which they are associated (black youth). A vivid example of this highly selective application [as cited by Andrew Rosenthal in *The New York Times*] took place during the 1992 presidential campaign when George W. Bush said "it was 'sick' to produce a record that he said glorified the killing of police officers, but saw no contradiction between this statement and his acceptance of support and endorsement from Arnold Schwarzenegger. As one [*New York Times*] reporter put it: "I stand against those who use films or records or television or video games to glorify killing law enforcement officers," said Mr. Bush, who counts among his top supporters the actor Arnold Schwarzenegger, whose character in the movies 'Terminator' and 'Terminator II: Judgment Day' kills or maims dozens of policemen."

Many critics of hip hop tend to interpret lyrics literally and as a direct reflection of the artist who performs them.

Popular Media Is Full of Violence

We live in a popular cultural world in which violent stories, images, lyrics, and performances occupy a wide cross-section of genres and mediums. Television shows such as *24* and *Law and Order*; Hollywood fare such as gangster, action, suspense, murder-driven, war, and horror films; video games; metal music; and novels—together, these comprise a diverse and highly accessible palate of violent images attached to compelling characters and bolstered by high-budget realistic sets and backdrops. Although anti-violence groups mention many of these genres and mediums, the bulk of the popular criticism about violence in popular culture is leveled at hip hop, and the fear-driven nature of the commentary is distinct from responses to the many other sources of violent imagery. There are three important differences between the criticisms of hip hop and rappers and those leveled at other music, films, shows, and videos—most of which, unlike rap music, are produced (not just consumed) primarily by whites.

First, hip hop gets extra attention for its violent content, and the *perception* of violence is heightened when it appears in rap music form rather than in some other popular genre of music featuring violent imagery. Rappers such as Lil' Jon, Ludacris, 50 Cent, and T.I. who claim that there is violence throughout popular culture and that they get overly singled out are right: Some violent imagery and lyrics in popular culture are responded to or perceived differently from others. Social psychologist Carrie B. Fried studied this issue and concluded that the perception of violence in rap music lyrics is affected by larger societal perceptions and stereotypes of African-Americans. In her study, she asked participants to respond to lyrics from a folk song about killing a police officer. To some of the participants the song was presented as rap; and to others, as country. Her study supports the hypothesis that lyrics presented as rap music are judged more harshly than the same lyrics presented as country music. She concluded that these identical lyrics seem more violent when featured in rap, perhaps because of the association of rap with the stereotypes of African-Americans.

Nevertheless, saying that there is violence elsewhere and that one is being unfairly singled out in connection with it isn't the best argument to make. Rappers' claims that violence is everywhere isn't a compelling case for hip hop's heightened investment in violent storytelling, especially for those of us who are worried about the extra levels of destructive forces working against poor black people. It is important, however, to pay close attention to the issue of unfair targeting, blame, and the compounded effect this perception of blacks as more violent has on black youth.

Interpreting Lyrics Literally

Second, many critics of hip hop tend to interpret lyrics literally and as a direct reflection of the artist who performs them. They equate rappers with thugs, see rappers as a threat to the larger society, and then use this "causal analysis" (that hip hop causes violence) to justify a variety of agendas: more police in black communities, more prisons to accommodate larger numbers of black and brown young people, and more censorship of expression. For these critics, hip hop is criminal propaganda. This literal approach, which extends beyond the individual to characterize an entire racial and class group, is rarely applied to violence-oriented mediums produced by whites.

Despite the caricature-like quality of many of hip hop's cultivated images and the similarity of many of its stories, critics often characterize rappers as speaking entirely autobiographically, implying that their stories of car-jacking, killing witnesses to crimes, hitting women, selling drugs, and beating up and killing opponents are statements of fact, truthful self-portraits. Thus, for instance, the rhyme in Lil' Wayne's "Damage Is Done" that describes him as running away with a "hammer in my jeans, dead body behind me, cops'll never find me" would be interpreted by many critics as a description of actual events. This assumption—that rappers are creating rhymed autobiographies—is the result of both rappers' own investment in perpetuating the idea that everything they say is true to their life experience (given that the genre has grown out of the African-American tradition of boasting in the first person) and the genre's investment in the pretense of no pretense. That is, the genre's promoters capitalize on the illusion that the artists are not performing but "keeping it real"—telling the truth, wearing outfits on stage that they'd wear in the street (no costumes), remaining exactly as they'd be if they were not famous, except richer. Part of this "keeping it real" ethos is a laudable effort to continue to identify with many of their fans, who don't see their style or life experiences represented anywhere else, from their own points of view; part of it is the result of conformity to the genre's conventions. It makes rappers more accessible, more reflective of some of the lived experiences and conditions that shape the lives of some of their fans. And it gives fans a sense that they themselves have the potential to reach celebrity status, to gain social value and prestige while remaining "true" to street life and culture, turning what traps them into an imagined gateway to success.

But this hyper-investment in the fiction of full-time autobiography in hip hop, especially for those artists who have adopted gangsta personas, has been exaggerated and distorted by a powerful history of racial images of black men as "naturally" violent and criminal. These false and racially motivated stereotypes were promoted throughout the last two centuries to justify both slavery and the violence, containment, and revised disenfranchisement that followed emancipation; and they persisted throughout the twentieth century to justify the development of urban segregation. In the early part of the twentieth century, well-respected scientists pursuing the "genetic" basis of racial and ethnic hierarchy embraced the view that blacks were biologically inferior, labeling them not only less intelligent but also more prone to crime and violence. These racial associations have been reinforced, directly and indirectly, through a variety of social outlets and institutions and, even today, continue to be circulated in contemporary scientific circles. In 2007, for example, Nobel laureate biologist Jim Watson said that he was "inherently gloomy about the prospects of Africa" because "all our social policies are based on the fact that their intelligence is the same as ours, whereas all the testing says not really." He went on to say that while he hoped everyone was equal, "people who have to deal with black employees find this is not true." And in the now-infamous, widely challenged 1994 book *The Bell Curve*, Richard J. Herrnstein and Charles Murray argued that it is highly likely that genes partly explain racial differences in IQ testing and intelligence and also claimed that intelligence is an important predictor of income, job performance, unwed pregnancy, and crime. Thus the pseudoscientific circle was closed: Blacks are genetically less intelligent, and intelligence level predicts income, performance, criminality, and sexually unsanctioned behavior; therefore, blacks are genetically disposed toward poverty, crime, and unwed motherhood.

This history of association of blacks with ignorance, sexual deviance, violence, and criminality has not only contributed to the believability of hip hop artists' fictitious autobiographical tales among fans from various racial groups but has also helped explain the excessive anxiety about the popularity and allure of these artists. The American public has long feared black criminality and violence as particularly anxiety-producing threats to whites—and the convincing "performance" of black criminality taps into these fears. So, both the voyeuristic pleasure of believing that hip hop artists are criminal minded and the exaggerated fear of them are deeply connected. Hip hop has successfully traded on this history of scientific racism and its imbedded impact on perceptions of poor black people, and has also been significantly criticized because of it.

Hip hop's violence is criticized at a heightened level and on different grounds from the vast array of violent images in American culture.

A Perceived Need to Protect Society from a Violent Culture

A third central difference between the criticism of hip hop and rappers and the criticism leveled at other forms of popular culture has to do with the way the artists themselves are perceived in relation to their audiences and to society. Hip hop's violence is criticized at a heightened level and on different grounds from the vast array of violent images in American culture, and these disparities in perception are very important. While heavy metal and other nonblack musical forms that contain substantial levels of violent imagery are likewise challenged by anti-violence critics, the operative assumption is that this music and its violence-peddling creators will negatively influence otherwise innocent listeners. Therefore (according to these critics), metal, video games, and violent movies influence otherwise nonviolent teenagers, encouraging them to act violently. From this perspective, "our youth" must be protected from these outside negative, aggressive influences.

Hip hop is not pure fiction or fantasy . . . , but neither is it unmediated reality and social advocacy for violence.

In the case of rap, the assumption is that the artists and their autobiographically styled lyrics represent an existing and already threatening violent black youth culture that must be prevented from affecting society at large. The [2002] quote from Bill O'Reilly . . . [about the rapper Ludacris endorsing Pepsi] reflects this approach. For O'Reilly, Ludacris is advocating violence and selling narcotics. Allowing him to be a representative for Pepsi would, as O'Reilly's logic goes, be similar to giving power to Pol Pot, the Cambodian leader of the brutal Khmer Rouge government, allowing a "subversive" guy access to legitimate power. This difference in interpretation—such that black rappers are viewed as leaders of an invading and destructively violent force that undermines society—has a dramatic effect on both the nature of the criticism and the larger perceptions of black youth that propel the ways in which they are treated. It sets the terms of how we respond, whom we police, and whom we protect.

Tales of violence in hip hop share important similarities with the overall investment in violence as entertainment (and political problem solving) in American culture, but they have more localized origins as well—namely, the damaging and terrible changes in black urban America over the past forty or so years. Although hip hop's penchant for stories with violent elements isn't purely a matter of documentary or autobiography, these stories are deeply connected to real social conditions and their impact on the lives of those who live them, close up. My point here may be confusing: On the one hand, I am saying that rappers are not the autobiographers they are often believed to be and that seeing them that way has contributed to the attacks they specifically face. But, on the other hand, I am also saying that much of what listeners hear in hip hop stories of violence is reflective of larger real-life social conditions. How can both be true?

Reality Lies Somewhere in the Middle

This is a crucial yet often improperly made distinction: Hip hop is not pure fiction or fantasy (such as might emerge from the mind of horror writer Stephen King), but neither is it unmediated reality and social advocacy for violence. Nor is rap a product of individual imagination (disconnected from lived experiences and social conditions) or sociological documentation or autobiography (an exact depiction of reality and personal action). Yet conversations about violence in hip hop strategically deploy both of these arguments. Defenders call it fiction, just like other artists' work, whereas critics want to emphasize rappers' own claims to be keeping it real as proof that these stories "advocate violence" or, as British politician David Cameron suggested, "[encourage] people to carry guns and knives."

Neither of these positions moves us toward a more empowering understanding of violent storytelling and imagery in hip hop or toward the fashioning of a productive, pro-youth position that recognizes the impact of these powerfully oppressive images without either accepting or excusing their negative effects. This is the line we must straddle: acknowledging the realities of discrimination and social policies that have created the conditions for the most dangerous and fractured black urban communities and, at the same time, not accepting or excusing the behaviors that are deeply connected to these local, social conditions.

The origins for the depth of investment in hip hop's myriad but context-specific stories involving guns, drugs, street culture, and crime are directly related to a combination of drastic changes in social life, community, and policies of neglect that destroyed neighborhood stability in much of black urban America. These local, social condition-based origins matter because the causal assumption that violent material when consumed increases violent actions underestimates the environmental forces at work. Although hip hop's violence has been marketed and exaggerated, its origins in violent urban communities and the reasons these communities became so violent must be understood. This context helps explain why hip hop's poorest inner-city fans and artists remain so invested in such stories. Rather than creating violence out of whole cloth, these stories are better understood as a distorted and profitable reflection of the everyday lives of too many poor black youth over the past forty or so years.

Context Is No Excuse but Must Be Considered

While context is crucial for explaining what we hear in a good deal of hip hop, context as justification for rap's constant repetition of violent storytelling is highly problematic. Rapper Tupac, for example, claimed that he was hoping to reveal the conditions in a powerful way to incite change: "I'm gonna show the most graphic details about what I see in my community and hopefully they'll stop it. Quick." Unfortunately, profits increased with increasingly violent, criminal-oriented rap while conditions remained and worsened. Despite the reality that these real conditions are not being changed because of rappers' stories and, instead, have become fodder for corporate profits, rappers continue to justify the use of black urban community distress and criminal icons along these lines, thus maintaining their value as a revenue stream. 50 Cent defended his lyrics, claiming that "[i]t's a reflection of the environment that I come from," and Jay-Z has confessed that "it's important for rappers to exaggerate 'life in the ghetto' because this is the only way the underclass can make its voice heard.". . .

The day-to-day violence that plagues poor communities must be taken into account both as a crucial context for explaining some of what we hear in hip hop and as a reality that compounds the power of violent storytelling. The allure of celebrities whose cachet depends partly on their relationship to a criminal/drug underworld is surely a form of social idolization that might encourage already-vulnerable kids to participate in the lucrative drug trade in neighborhoods where good-paying jobs are nearly nonexistent. A good deal of 50 Cent's initial promotional campaign relied on the fact that he sold crack, that his mother was a crack user, that he was shot nine times and wore a bulletproof vest to protect him against enemies. We can't constantly make violence sexy for young people who find themselves mired in violent social spaces that are mostly not of their making and then expect them not to valorize violent action.

The Rap Music Industry Exploits Violence for Profit

L. Brent Bozell III

L. Brent Bozell III is the president of the Media Research Center, a conservative media watchdog organization.

On Sept. 25, [2007] the House Subcommittee on Commerce, Trade and Consumer Protection, chaired by Bobby Rush, D-Ill., held a very unique hearing, focusing on the way the culture is being soured by the makers of sexist and racially charged rap music. Inspired by the furor over fired radio host Don Imus and his "ho" talk, the hearing was titled "From Imus to Industry: The Business of Stereotypes and Degrading Images."

That's a great title. For years now, record companies have made untold millions of dollars spreading a message glorifying the thug life, preaching greed and lust, and portraying women as nothing more than pornographic mannequins. From the debate that emerged on Capitol Hill, it's very easy to find the winners and the losers.

Winner: Bobby Rush. The congressman could have knuckled under from pressure by the anything-goes Old Guard of gangsta rap, but instead he boldly put his prestige where his heart is. He said this music of violence and degradation has "reduced too many of our youngsters to automatons, those who don't recognize life, those who don't value life."

He was unequivocal. "There is a problem—a deep-seated, deeply rooted problem in our country," he said. "The paycheck is not an excuse for being part of the problem."

Loser: Michael Eric Dyson. The professor and Bill Cosby-hating author has become America's leading excuse-maker for

L. Brent Bozell III, "Congress vs. Gangsta Rap," Creators.com, 2007. By permission of L. Brent Bozell and Creators Syndicate, Inc.

irresponsible thug music. He blamed America, that never-draining cesspool of racism, for whatever problem exists. "America is built upon degrading images of black men and women, so any discussion of misogyny or homophobia or sexism has got to dig deep into America, including Congress and corporate and religious institutions."

[Bobby Rush] understands black rage against injustice in America, but in no way does it justify thuggery.

A Higher Responsibility

Rush was not accepting that ridiculous excuse. He understands black rage against injustice in America, but in no way does it justify thuggery. He said: "I still have rage, but how do I channel it? Am I going to spew out counterproductively? Or do I accept a higher responsibility to take my rage and do something to improve the community?"

Winner: Master P. The former gangsta-rapper (his real name is Percy Miller) came to Congress and apologized for his musical transgressions. The angry music of his past, he said, came from seeing relatives and friends shot and killed.

But he said now he doesn't even want his own children to listen to his music, "so if I can do anything to change this, I'm going to take a stand and do that." He also apologized to women for his music. "I was honestly wrong."

Later on NPR, he explained that listening to other gangsta-rappers "inspired" his own violent lyrics, like Ice-T boasting, "I am a nightmare stalking, psychopath walking." He said that song "put me in the mood when I was in the ghetto just to continuously make music like that." It was inspiring that he mustered the fortitude to confess before Congress.

Loser: David Banner. This rapper with the "Incredible Hulk" stage name (real name: Levell Crump) lived up to his rage-spewing image. He blamed everyone else for his own disgusting lyrics. "Hip-hop is sick because America is sick," he said. "Change the situation in my neighborhood, and maybe I'll get better."

But of course Crump doesn't really want to get better or do better. He wants to continue trotting out the usual poet-of-the-streets bilge: "Rap music is the voice of the underbelly of America. In most cases, America wants to hide the negative that it does to its people. Hip hop is the voice, and how dare America not give us the opportunity to be heard!"

The Music Industry Is Culpable

Loser: the music-selling conglomerates. Corporate officials sitting before Congress were unafraid to stand up for lyrics extolling profanity, criminality and sexism. Asked if explicit lyrics by rapper 50 Cent constituted free speech, Doug Morris of Universal Music proclaimed: "Yes. It is not my place in life to tell him what to say."

Warner Music boss Edgar Bronfman said tasteless language "is in the eye of the beholder." (Tell that to Don Imus.) And Phillippe Dauman, the president of Viacom (think MTV and BET), extolled the scummy street poetry: "We have a responsibility to speak authentically to our viewers." Viacom should be authentically rejected by consumers.

Violent Rap Lyrics Make Listeners More Accepting of Violence

Karen Dill

Media violence researcher Karen Dill is an associate professor of psychology in the School of Social and Behavioral Sciences at Lenoir-Rhyne College in North Carolina.

I am Dr. Karen Dill and have been conducting research in the field of media psychology since 1994. My specialization is in media violence, violence against women, video games, and stereotyping of women and minorities in the media. In this capacity, I have co-authored a statement on interactive media violence which led to the American Psychological Association's (APA) Resolution on Violence in Video Games and Interactive Media, adopted in 2005. In addition, I currently serve on the APA committee on Interactive Media and have published in the field of media psychology with an emphasis on video games, violence and gender stereotypes. My dissertation, *Video Games and Aggressive Thoughts, Feelings and Behaviors in the Laboratory and in Life*, co-authored with my mentor Dr. Craig Anderson, is the single most-cited research paper on video game violence effects.

Americans spend two-thirds of our waking lives consuming mass media. Be it television, movies, music, video games or the internet, media consumption is the number one activity of choice for Americans—commanding, on average, 3,700 hours of each citizen's time annually. The average American

Karen Dill, Testimony before the House Subcommittee on Commerce, Trade and Consumer Protection, Subcommittee on Commerce, Trade and Consumer Protection, "From Imus to Industry: The Business of Stereotypes and Degrading Images," House Committee on Energy and Commerce, United States House of Representatives, Sept. 25, 2007.

child devotes 45 hours per week to media consumption, more time than she spends in school.

How Mass Media Shapes Culture

Since culture is our shared reality, created and sustained through common experience, American culture is now largely that which is shaped and maintained by the mass media. Television, video games, music and other forms of media create meaning including shared beliefs, values and rules. Television, games, songs and movies tell stories, project images and communicate ideas. Since we are social creatures, it is natural for us to learn who we are, how we should act, feel, think and believe through the stories of our common culture.

Violent music lyrics have been shown to increase aggressive thoughts and feelings.

This creation of culture through popular media was sadly exemplified recently when radio personality Don Imus referred to a college women's basketball team as "nappy-headed ho's." Sadder still, many responded that the racist and sexist language was acceptable because that type of language is used by minorities in rap music. Unfortunately racist and sexist slurs influence real people, for example sending the message to girls that this is how our society views them and causing issues with self esteem and identity.

The Psychology Behind Media

When people say that media messages do not matter, they do not understand the psychology behind the media. For example, research on the third person effect has shown repeatedly that people believe that they themselves are immune to being affected by negative media content such as media violence, but that they believe other people, especially children, are affected. A recent study showed that the more violent video games you play, the less likely you are to believe that you are affected by video game violence. Reasons for these misperceptions include 1) the natural tendency to reject the notion that our habits are harmful; 2) a mistaken view of how media effects work (e.g., that media violence effects are always immediately observable and extreme such as murder); and 3) that media are produced primarily to entertain us (rather than to make a profit); and 4) that media do not affect the viewer (including the tendency to believe that important effects such as violence must have an important cause, not a trivial cause such as watching television).

Research on music has demonstrated that exposure to violent rap videos increases adversarial sexual beliefs (viewing men and women as enemies in the sexual sphere), negative mood, and acceptance of relationship violence (for example, believing it is acceptable for a boyfriend to shove his girlfriend out of jealousy). Additionally, violent music lyrics have been shown to increase aggressive thoughts and feelings. Across a number of studies in which researchers controlled for artist, style and other relevant factors, results showed conclusively that it was the aggressive content that caused the observed changes. . . .

The Need for Regulation

We enjoy freedom of expression in this country, but no country can grant us freedom from consequences. Scientists call it cause and effect. To put it more poetically, you reap what you sow. If you want peace, plant peace. If you want justice, grow justice. If we plant the seeds of violence and hate, we, as a culture, will reap what we have sown.

My message today is that violence, hatred, racism and sexism in the media do matter. One way our government can ameliorate this situation is to act on the research findings by planning legislation and regulation accordingly. Beyond that, we have a dire need in our schools to implement a curriculum that teaches how the media work (known as media literacy training) so that if a child hears these messages she is better equipped to deal with them. We need to make our priorities protecting and empowering children and all people rather than placing emphasis on protecting the rights of special interests to profit from selling messages of hate and injustice. We also need to recognize the deception involved with defending these harmful messages as freedom of expression.

Violent Rap Lyrics Do Not Affect Listener Behavior or Attitudes

Jennifer Copley

Researcher and editor Jennifer Copley is a regular contributor to Suite 101, a Canadian website.

Many parents are alarmed when they discover that their children have developed a taste for rap music, but is there really any reason for concern?

Studies have been conducted to assess the effects of listening to rap music on teenagers and young adults. Findings thus far are mixed, but overall they suggest that listening to rap music does not cause aggressive or deviant behaviour.

One study found that young subjects who watched violent rap videos were more accepting of violent actions, particularly against women. Additionally, those who watched either violent or nonviolent rap videos were more inclined to express materialistic attitudes and favor potentially acquiring possessions through crime, as well as holding more negative views on the likelihood of succeeding through academic pursuits.

Another study found that adolescent females, after watching a rap video depicting women in sexually subordinate roles, were more inclined to express acceptance of violence against women in a dating situation. However, increased acceptance of crime and violence appears to be linked with viewing violent or sexist rap videos rather than listening to rap music on its own.

Young men who had little previous exposure to rap music were the subjects of an experiment in which researchers had

Jennifer Copley, "Rap Music's Psychological Effects: Research into Mood, Behavior, Crime, Violence and Gender Relations," *Suite 101*, May 8, 2008. jennifercopley.suite101.com. Copyright © 2008 by Jennifer Copley.

one group listen to rap music with lyrics, another listen to rap music without lyrics, a third just read the lyrics, and a fourth group neither listen nor read. After the exposure, none of the subjects held more negative attitudes toward women, but those who read or heard the lyrics were more inclined to express adversarial sexual beliefs.

As would be expected, only rap music with misogynistic themes appears to create misogynistic attitudes and greater acceptance of violence against women. Other types of rap do not have a negative effect on the perception of women.

Behavioral Problems and Academic Achievement

Although research has found a correlation between preference for heavy metal or rap music and behavioral problems, drug or alcohol use, arrests and sexual promiscuity, these behavioral problems usually begin before students begin listening to rap or heavy metal, which indicates that the music does not cause behavioral problems or addiction. Rather, it suggests that at-risk youth are more inclined to prefer heavy metal or rap music.

Only rap music with misogynistic themes appears to create misogynistic attitudes and greater acceptance of violence against women.

While a number of studies have associated lower grades with students who listen to rap or heavy metal music, one study found that white students actually improved their academic abilities after watching rap videos, as well as expressing more progressive attitudes—after watching politically focused rap videos, they were more inclined to support a liberal black political candidate. Unfortunately, there was no indication of similar research being conducted with black students.

Listening to rap or heavy metal has not been shown to increase suicidal ideation and anxiety or adversely affect self-esteem among college-aged men and women. Oddly enough, students listening to a nonviolent rap song experienced more depressive symptoms than those who listened to a violent rap song. Overall, rap songs are more inclined to generate angry emotions than heavy metal songs, however.

Assumptions About Rap Music

Some research suggests that people may ascribe negative effects to rap due to subconscious racism. Subjects who were given a violent lyrical passage were more inclined to rate it as dangerous or offensive if they believed it came from a rap song than if they were told that it originated from a country music song.

In Marseille, France, rap and hip hop are thriving musical forms, and many residents believe that the positive effects of this music are the reason poor North African neighborhoods in the region have not suffered the rioting seen in other areas of Paris.

Overall, there is no consistent evidence that rap music on its own (without videos) significantly influences behaviors or attitudes. Also, while those who are not fans of rap tend to assume that all songs in the genre focus on violent, criminal or misogynistic themes, in reality, rap is a diverse genre, with many artists addressing important socio-political issues and positive themes, so all rap music cannot be lumped together in a single category.

References:

- Carrie, F. (1999). "Who's afraid of rap: Differential reactions to music lyrics." *Journal of Applied Social Psychology*, 29(4), 705–721.

- Cobb, M.D., & Boettcher, III, W.A. (2007). "Ambivalent sexism and misogynistic rap music: Does exposure to Eminem increase sexism?" *Journal of Applied Social Psychology*, 37(12), 3025–3042.

- Johnson, J.D.; Jackson, L.A.; & Gatto, L. (1995). "Violent attitudes and deferred academic aspirations: Deleterious effects of exposure to rap music." Basic & *Applied Social Psychology*, 16(1/2), 27–41.

- Kimmelman, M. (19 December 2007). "In Marseille, rap helps keep the peace." *New York Times*, 157(54163), E1–E5.

- Tatum, B.L. (1999). "The link between rap music and youth crime and violence: A review of the literature and issues [HTML Version]." *Justice Professional*, 11(3).

- Wester, S.R.; Crown, C.L.; Quatman, G.L.; & Heesacker, M. (1997). "The influence of sexually violent rap music on attitudes of men with little prior exposure." *Psychology of Women Quarterly*, 21(4), 497.

Gangsta Rappers Can Be Effective Violence Prevention Messengers

Shoshana Walter

Shoshana Walter is the crime reporter for The Bay Citizen, *a nonprofit, nonpartisan, member-supported news organization based in the San Francisco Bay Area.*

Last weekend [February 2012], the Oakland rapper Philthy Rich, who is on probation for firearms possession, was arrested on charges of driving an allegedly stolen Bentley. He posted $30,000 bail.

Then he made plans to speak at an elementary school in support of nonviolence.

In a past era, youth mentors were expected to have squeaky-clean records. But Philthy Rich, whose birth name is Philip Beasley, is among a new generation of role models who are being welcomed into community outreach organizations. Their credibility with young people, these groups say, is bolstered by their experience growing up in Oakland's high-crime neighborhoods, including run-ins with the law.

Philthy Rich has become a high-profile spokesman for local violence-prevention efforts. His arrest highlights a difference in perceptions between many police officers and leaders of nonprofit groups who are eager to reach jaded inner-city youth. Community organizers say young people can relate to rappers like Philthy Rich. The police simply consider Philthy Rich a criminal.

Shoshana Walter, "'Unlikely Messengers' for Violence Prevention—A criminal record no longer means you can't be a mentor," *The Bay Citizen*, February 18, 2012. This piece was produced by The Bay Citizen, a part of the nonprofit Center for Investigative Reporting. For more information visit baycitizen.org. Contact the reporter at swalter@baycitizen.org.

"One of our strategies is the use of unlikely messengers," said Nicole Lee, executive director of the Urban Peace Movement, a violence-prevention organization.

"It's predictable that I'm going to tell them to stop the violence," she said. "But I haven't lived the life that Philthy Rich has."

A Rapper's Rap Sheet

In his music, Philthy Rich, 29, is boastful and blunt, borrowing from tragic memories of his youth in the Seminary in East Oakland, a neighborhood rife with guns and drugs. He grew up without his father and bounced frequently between homes. His first arrest, he said, was when he was 11, after he beat up another child and stole his bicycle. In 2007, he was arrested for selling cocaine.

In 2009, as he and his cousin were attending the memorial for a friend killed in a shooting, someone opened fire. His cousin, an aspiring police officer, was killed.

In his music, Philthy Rich, 29, is boastful and blunt, borrowing from tragic memories of his youth.

A natural self-promoter, Philthy Rich spoke of his cousin's death and a dozen others on an episode of the Discovery Channel's "Gang Wars." He said he was done selling drugs, and teamed up with Lee and rappers and nonprofit groups to produce a CD called "Turf Unity." Several months later, he was arrested for illegal firearms possession. He said he was carrying a pistol for protection.

But his criminal background did not dissuade Lee and others from entrusting Philthy Rich with their message of nonviolence. Like the rapper, young people eager for protection in Oakland's high-crime areas find it very easy to obtain illegal guns, she said.

"Our approach is really about meeting people where they are," Lee said.

This philosophy is shared across the city, particularly in areas with high concentrations of poverty and violence.

Many Oakland police officers view these programs as condoning lawlessness.

Street Outreach

The City of Oakland's street-outreach team, a group that walks the city's crime hot spots, includes several former gang members. Some 60 to 70 percent of the young people hired by Youth Uprising, an East Oakland nonprofit group, have criminal records, said Olis Simmons, the group's executive director.

That high proportion is "not coincidental," Simmons said. "I go after them. Hell, somebody's got to hire them. If you can turn them around, you turn the neighborhood around."

Many Oakland police officers view these programs as condoning lawlessness. "It's turned into a network of mediocre criminals," one homicide detective said about Youth Uprising. (The officer spoke on condition of anonymity because he is not authorized to speak to the news media.)

In 2010, when Too Short, the iconic Oakland rapper, was serving as a Youth Uprising counselor, he was charged with assaulting security guards at one of his shows in Idaho. The same year, another Youth Uprising employee was charged with murder and robbery.

For his part, Philthy Rich said he owned the car he was arrested in and planned to show a judge the registration papers to prove it. But he admitted that his criminal record made him an unlikely candidate for a youth mentor.

"At first it was hard, because I didn't want to get up there, cursing and saying stop the violence, and then get up there and rap about the violence," Philthy Rich said about his first performance at Youth Uprising. "Now I feel comfortable doing me."

Organizations to Contact

The editors have compiled the following list of organizations concerned with the issues debated in this book. The descriptions are derived from materials provided by the organizations. All have publications or information available for interested readers. The list was compiled on the date of publication of the present volume; names, addresses, phone and fax numbers, and e-mail and Internet addresses may change. Be aware that many organizations take several weeks or longer to respond to inquiries, so allow as much time as possible.

Allhiphop.com
244 Fifth Ave., Suite 2528, New York, NY 10001
(877) 499-5111
e-mail: grouchygreg@tmail.com
website: http://allhiphop.com

Allhiphop.com was founded in 1998 as a resource for hip-hop artists and fans on the Internet and has grown to be the world's biggest hip-hop website with more than five million visitors a month. The site features daily news, interviews, reviews, multimedia, and a variety of hip-hop community forums with which visitors can participate. Users can also sign up to receive news updates via text message or e-mail. The website's extensive archive includes the essays "The Gentrification of Rap: Did Hip-Hop Sell Us Out?", "Fear of an Intelligent Black Man: Does Hip-Hop Hate the Educated Rapper?", and "Iz Blak Peeple Stoopid? Rap and the Racial Inferiority Myth."

Concerned Women of America (CWA)
1015 Fifteenth St., Suite 1100, Washington, DC 20005
(202) 488-7000 • fax: (202) 448-0806
e-mail: mail@cwfa.org
website: www.cwfa.org

Concerned Women of America (CWA) seeks to protect the interests of American families, promote biblical values, and provide a voice throughout the United States for women who believe in Judeo-Christian values. CWA believes that sexually explicit popular culture contributes to the decline of families and interferes with raising healthy children. CWA publishes the bimonthly *Family Voice* and numerous press releases and reports, including "Sexually Explicit Media and Children" and "Music's Deadly Influence."

Crunk Feminist Collective (CFC)
e-mail: crunkfeminists@gmail.com
website: http://crunkfeministcollective.wordpress.com

The Crunk Feminist Collective (CFC) is an online blog community that provides a forum for women and men of color who came of age in the Hip-Hop Generation and seek to articulate a crunk feminist consciousness. Postings are made by scholars-activists from various professions who share a commitment to nurturing and sustaining one another through progressive feminist visions. Crunk music blends hip-hop culture and southern black culture; the term is used to describe the increasingly popular style of southern rap and hip-hop.

Culture Shock
2110 Hancock St., Suite 200, San Diego, CA   92110
(619) 299-2110 • fax: (619) 299-2666
website: www.cultureshockdance.org

Culture Shock is a nonprofit hip-hop dance troupe dedicated to offering children and youth in diverse communities an alternative to street life by providing a rewarding activity and instilling confidence. Founded in 1993, Culture Shock has spread from its home location of San Diego, California, to cities across the United States, Canada, and the United Kingdom.

The Heritage Foundation
214 Massachusetts Ave. NE, Washington, DC   20002-4999
(800) 544-4843 • fax: (202) 546-8328

e-mail: info@heritage.org
website: www.heritage.org

The Heritage Foundation is a conservative public policy organization dedicated to individual liberty, free-market principles,
and limited government. It advises parents to restrict the music and movies that their children and youth consume. Its
resident scholars publish position papers on a wide range of
issues, including such titles as "A Culture Awash in Porn" and
"The Culture War: A Five-Point Plan for Parents."

Hip-Hop Association (H2A)
545 Eighth Ave., 10th Floor, New York, NY   10018
(718) 682-2744
e-mail: info@hiphopassociation.org
website: www.hiphopassociation.org

Founded in 2002, the Hip-Hop Association (H2A) works to
facilitate critical thinking and foster constructive social change
and unity. It seeks to promote tolerance, civic participation,
social reform, and economic sustainability, while advancing
hip-hop culture through innovative programming. H2A organizes an international film festival and publishes the monthly
Defuse News, which includes commentary, announcements,
and resources such as information about grants, fellowships,
and job opportunities.

The Hip Hop Caucus
1112 Sixteenth St. NW, Suite 110, Washington, DC   20036
(202) 293-5902
e-mail: contact@hiphopcaucus.org
website: http://hiphopcaucus.org

Founded in 2004, the Hip Hop Caucus works with celebrity,
media, and entertainment partners to mobilize, educate, and
engage young people on the social issues that directly affect
their lives and communities. The group organizes young
people to be active in elections, policymaking, and service
projects, and it works to inform and move the urban commu-

nity to action. Its programs include the Gulf Coast Renewal campaign to advocate for survivors of Hurricane Katrina, the Make Hip Hop Not War campaign to involve youth in the peace movement, and the Respect My Vote! campaign, a non-partisan voter registration and education effort.

Hip Hop Congress
e-mail: shamako@hiphopcongress.com
website: www.hiphopcongress.com

The Hip Hop Congress is a nonprofit with the mission to use hip-hop culture to inspire young people to get involved in so-cial action, civic service, and cultural creativity. The organiza-tion is the product of a merger of artists and students and has more than thirty chapters in the United States and throughout Europe and Africa. Its Artist Program helps artists pool re-sources, sell music, and take advantage of music industry op-portunities, without giving away the rights to their works. The Hip Hop Congress also works to organize and support an Ur-ban Teacher Network (UTN) where educators and youth men-tors share ideas and curriculum and build after-school extra-curricular and mentor programs for the youth whom they teach. The organization's website includes information about its various programs and chapter activities and articles related to hip-hop.

Hip-Hop Summit Action Network (HSAN)
e-mail: info@hsan.org
website: www.hsan.org

Founded in 2001 by Def Jam records founder Russell Sim-mons, the Hip-Hop Summit Action Network (HSAN) is dedi-cated to harnessing the cultural relevance of hip-hop music to serve as a catalyst for education advocacy and other societal concerns fundamental to the empowerment of youth. HSAN is a nonprofit, nonpartisan national coalition of hip-hop art-ists, entertainment industry leaders, education advocates, civil rights proponents, and youth leaders united in the belief that hip-hop is an enormously influential agent for social change.

The organization's website includes information about its various programs and an extensive archive of articles related to hip-hop and rap.

Hip Hop Theater Festival (HHTF)
442-D Lorimer St., No. 195, Brooklyn, NY   11206
(718) 497-4282 • fax: (718) 497-4240
e-mail: info@hhtf.org
website: www.hiphoptheaterfest.org

The mission of Hip Hop Theater Festival (HHTF) is to promote hip-hop theater as a recognized genre by commissioning and developing new work and helping artists collaborate and build networks with other artists and institutions around the United States and internationally. The organization presents live events created by artists who combine a variety of theatrical forms, including dance, spoken word, and live music. HHTF also strives to bring new, younger audiences to the theater in large numbers, in an effort to ensure the future of live performance.

Morality in Media (MIM)
1100 G St. NW, No. 450, Washington, DC   20005
(212) 393-7245
e-mail: mim@moralityinmedia.org
website: www.moralityinmedia.org

Founded in 1962, Morality in Media (MIM) is an interfaith organization that fights pornography and opposes indecency in mainstream media. It maintains the National Obscenity Law Center, a clearinghouse of legal materials on obscenity law. MIM publishes the bimonthlies *Morality in Media* and *Obscenity Law Bulletin* and has published several papers, including "Hip-Hop Misogyny: A Destructive Force," "Altered Perceptions—Media and Youth," and "Mass Murder and Popular Culture."

National Congress of Black Women (NCBW)
1251 Fourth St. SW, Washington, DC   20024

(202) 678-6788
e-mail: info@nationalcongressbw.org
website: www.nationalcongressbw.org

The National Congress of Black Women (NCBW) supports the advancement of African American women in politics and government. The congress also engages in research on critical issues that affect the quality of life of African American women and youth. Through its Commission on Entertainment, the NCBW campaigns against the glorification of violence, misogyny, pornography, and drugs in popular entertainment. It publishes project reports on its website, one of which is "Crusading Against Gangsta/Porno Rap."

Bibliography

Books

H. Samy Alim, Awad Ibrahim, and Alastair Pennycook, eds.
Global Linguistic Flows: Hip Hop Cultures, Youth Identities, and the Politics of Language. New York: Routledge, 2009.

Molefi K. Asante Jr.
It's Bigger than Hip Hop: The Rise of the Post-Hip-Hop Generation. New York: St. Martin's Press, 2008.

Dipannita Basu and Sidney J. Lemelle, eds.
The Vinyl Ain't Final: Hip Hop and the Globalization of Black Popular Culture. London: Pluto Press, 2006.

Raquel Cepeda, ed.
And It Don't Stop! The Best American Hip-Hop Journalism of the Last 25 Years. New York: Faber and Faber, 2004.

Jeff Chang
Can't Stop, Won't Stop: A History of the Hip-Hop Generation. New York: Picador/St. Martin's Press, 2005.

Dan Charnas
The Big Payback: The History of the Business of Hip-Hop. New York: New American Library Trade, 2011.

Michael Eric Dyson
Holler If You Hear Me: Searching for Tupac Shakur. New York: Basic Civitas Books/Perseus Books Group, 2003.

Murray Forman and Mark Anthony Neal, eds.	*That's the Joint! The Hip-Hop Studies Reader*, 2nd ed. New York: Routledge, 2012.
Mickey Hess	*Is Hip Hop Dead? The Past, Present, and Future of America's Most Wanted Music.* Westport, CT: Praeger, 2007.
Bakari Kitwana	*The Hip Hop Generation: Young Blacks and the Crisis in African American Culture.* New York: Basic Civitas Books/Perseus Book Group, 2002.
Bakari Kitwana	*Why White Kids Love Hip Hop: Wankstas, Wiggers, Wannabes, and the New Reality of Race in America.* New York: Basic Civitas Books/ Perseus Book Group, 2005.
Mark Anthony Neal	*What the Music Said: Black Popular Music and Black Public Culture.* New York: Routledge, 1999.
Jeffrey O. G. Ogbar	*Hip-Hop Revolution: The Culture and Politics of Rap.* Lawrence: University Press of Kansas, 2007.
Imani Perry	*Prophets of the Hood: Politics and Poetics in Hip Hop.* Durham, NC: Duke University Press, 2004.
Gwendolyn D. Pough	*Check It While I Wreck It: Black Womanhood, Hip-Hop Culture, and the Public Sphere.* Boston: Northeastern University Press, 2004.

Eithne Quinn — *Nuthin' but a "G" Thang: The Culture and Commerce of Gangsta Rap.* New York: Columbia University Press, 2005.

T. Denean Sharpley-Whiting — *Pimps Up, Ho's Down: Hip Hop's Hold on Young Black Women.* New York: New York University Press, 2007.

Steve Stoute — *The Tanning of America: How Hip-Hop Created a Culture That Rewrote the Rules of the New Economy.* New York: Gotham, 2011.

S. Craig Watkins — *Hip Hop Matters: Politics, Pop Culture, and the Struggle for the Soul of a Movement.* Boston: Beacon Press, 2005.

Ben Westhoff — *Dirty South: OutKast, Lil Wayne, Soulja Boy, and the Southern Rappers Who Reinvented Hip-Hop.* Chicago: Chicago Review Press, 2011.

Periodicals and Internet Sources

William Lee Adams — "Ivory Tower: Teachings of Tupac," *Newsweek*, October 4, 2004.

Craig A. Anderson, Nicholas L. Carnagey, and Janie Eubanks — "Exposure to Violent Media: The Effects of Songs with Violent Lyrics on Aggressive Thoughts and Feelings," *Journal of Personality and Social Psychology*, Vol. 84, No. 5, 2003.

Adam Bradley   "One Nation Under Hip-Hop; Even
                      as Its Beat Begins to Fade, the
                      Influence of the Music Is
                      Everywhere," *Washington Post*,
                      January 28, 2007.

Ed Caesar   "Are Rap Artists Responsible for the
                      Explosion of Gang Culture? The Big
                      Question," *The Independent*
                      (London), August 10, 2007.

Delman Coates   "The Rap on BET: BET's Apologists
                      Twist Facts," *Atlanta
                      Journal-Constitution*, October 14,
                      2007.

Hillary Crosley   "Rapper-cussions? Rap Artists/Execs
                      Discuss Hip-Hop Music and Imus,"
                      Billboard.biz, April 28, 2007.
                      www.billboard.biz/bbbiz/home.

Stanley Crouch   "Hip Hop's Inner Demons Add Fuel
                      to the Fight," *Daily News* (New York),
                      July 2, 2007. www.nydailynews.com.

Gilbert Cruz   "Thursday Q&A: Tricia Rose, Author
                      of *The Hip Hop Wars*," *Time*,
                      December 11, 2008.

Liz Essley   "Engaging Pupils Through Hip-hop,"
                      Washington Times, June 15, 2009.

Reyhan Harmanci   "Academic Hip-Hop? Yes, Yes Y'all,"
                      San Francisco Chronicle, March 5,
                      2007. www.sfgate.com.

Hamil R. Harris   "Hip-hop Moves from Street to
                      Pulpit in Youth Outreach,"
                      Washington Post, November 7, 2011.

Hua Hsu   "The End of White America?" *The
                           Atlantic*, January/February 2009.
                           www.theatlantic.com.

Tim Johnson   "Hip-hop, Texting May Help Save
                           World's Languages," McClatchy, June
                           27, 2011. www.mcclatchydc.com.

Bushra Juhi   "Rap, Tattoos, Hoodies: Part of U.S.
                           Legacy in Iraq," *Seattle Times*,
                           November 23, 2011.
                           http://seattletimes.com.

Jenny Mayo   "Hip-Hop's Faithful; Praise Lyrics
                           with Rap Beat Gain Youth Cred,"
                           Washington Times, May 16, 2008.

John H.   "How Hip-hop Holds Blacks Back,"
McWhorter   *City Journal*, Summer 2003.
                           www.city-journal.org.

Nekesa Mumbi   "Rappers Cleaning Up Lyrics
Moody   Post-Imus," *Washington Post*, August
                           2, 2007. www.washingtonpost.com.

Amanda   "Musical Trafficking: Urban Youth
Morrison   and the Narcocorrido-Hardcore Rap
                           Nexus," *Western Folklore* Vol. 67, No.
                           4, Fall 2008.

National Public   "Obama Hip-Hop: From Mixtapes to
Radio   Mainstream," November 7, 2008.
                           www.npr.org.

Tara Parker-Pope   "Under the Influence of . . . Music?"
                           New York Times, February 5, 2008.
                           http://well.blogs.nytimes.com.

Amanda Paulson   "Misogyny—Set to Music—May
                   Alter Teen Behavior," *Christian
                   Science Monitor*, August 8, 2006.
                   www.csmonitor.com.

Thaddeus Russell   "Is Rap Tomorrow's Jazz?" *Los
                   Angeles Times*, August 16, 2005.

Kelefa Sanneh   "Don't Blame Hip-hop," *New York
                   Times*, April 25, 2007.
                   www.nytimes.com.

Reed Shackelford   "Bad Influence or Good Music?
                   Hip-hop Takes Away Human Dignity,
                   Degrades Women," *The Advocate*,
                   October 24, 2008.

T. Denean   "Pimpin' Ain't Easy: Hip-hop's
Sharpley-Whiting   Relationship to Young Women Is
                   Complicated, Varied and Helping to
                   Shape a New Black Gender Politics,"
                   Colorlines Magazine, May/June 2007.

Toure   "Challenging Hip-Hop's Masculine
                   Ideal," *New York Times*, December 25,
                   2011. www.nytimes.com.

Jimmy Wang   "Now Hip-Hop, Too, Is Made in
                   China," *New York Times*, January 24,
                   2009. www.nytimes.com.

Jeff Weiss   "Has the L.A. Hip-Hop Plague
                   Finally Passed?" *LA Weekly*,
                   September 25, 2008.
                   www.laweekly.com.

Index

A

Accel Partners, 93
Aerosmith (rock group), 71
African American culture
  black feminism, 110–111
  black identity, 83–84
  hip hop as crossover music,
    94–95
  hip-hop feminism, 108–113
  influence on hip hop, 29–31,
    33
  rap music and black identity,
    83–84
  rap music as literary art form,
    46–49
  rap music harmful to, 55–60
  stereotypes of, 124
African American English (AAE),
  31
Afrika Bambaataa (rap artist), 78,
  93
Afrocentrists, 74
Akinwole-Bandele, Lumumba, 118
Akinyele (rap artist), 108
Algeria, 17, 26, 40
Allen, Harry, 71
American Psychological
  Association's (APA) Resolution
  on Violence in Video Games, 135
Anderson, Benedict, 23–24
Anderson, Craig, 135
Antisocial elements of hip hop, 95
Anti-violence groups, 123, 127–
  128
Arabian Knightz (hip hop group),
  16, 26

Arab rap music, 16–17, 39–40
Arab Spring uprisings, 16, 17
Asen, Joshua, 17
Ashhurst, Carmen, 72–74
Australasian youth culture, 33

B

Bahrain, 17
Baker, Rob, 78
Balance the Airwaves Campaign,
  78
Banner, David, 133–134
BBC World Service, 16
B-boying element of hip hop, 71
Beasley, Philip, 143
Beastie Boys (rap group), 33
The Bell Curve (Herrnstein), 126
Ben Ali, Zine El Abidine, 16, 25–
  26, 39
Ben Amor, Hamada. *See* El
  Général
Bennett, Dionne, 22–31
Beyond Beats & Rhymes (film), 75
Black Entertainment Television
  (BET), 38, 59, 74–75, 105
Black feminism, 110–111
Black identity, 22, 83–84
Blackmon, Dereca, 116
Bling Shopping Network, 74
Boogie Down Productions (rap
  group), 44
Bouazizi, Mohamed, 25
Bozell, L. Brent, III, 132–134
Brathwaite, Fred, 93

Breakdancing, 22, 32, 52, 71, 83, 92
Brewer, Craig, 64–65
Bronfman, Edgar, Jr., 99, 134
Brown, James, 45, 71
Bryan (Baby) Williams (rap artist), 74
Bush, George W., 76, 85, 122–123
B-word (bitch) usage, 37, 52, 54, 59, 64, 104

C

Cambodia, 19
Cameron, David, 129
Campaign Against Violence, 78
Canada, 38
Carson, Keith, 115–116
Carter, Shawn (Jay-Z), 32–33, 83
Casey, Rashawn, 106
Castro, Fidel, 34
Celemencki, Jacqueline, 51, 52
Chang, Jeff, 69–80
Chapman, Duane, 37
Chavis, Benjamin, 79–80, 98
Christian Rap, 35
Chuck D (rap artist), 33, 72
Citizen Change Campaign, 76
Clear Channel radio, 74, 78
Clemente, Rosa, 117
Clinton, Bill, 76
Clinton, Hillary, 84, 85
Code-switching practices, 31
Cohen, Lyor, 79, 99
Cold Crush Brothers (rap group), 72
Combs, Sean. *See* Sean (P. Diddy) Combs
Commercialized rap, 18–19

Common (rap artist), 88
Confessions of a Video Vixen (Steffans), 104
Cooper, Anna Julia, 103
Copley, Jennifer, 139–142
Cosby, Bill, 106, 133
Crazy Legs (rap artist), 93
Crump, Levell, 133–134
Cuba, 34

D

Dauman, Phillippe, 134
Davey D (hip hop activist), 114–118
El Deeb (rap artist), 16, 19, 41–42
Deejaying (DJing), 22, 71, 83, 92
Def Jam (rap group), 72, 73–75, 98
Democratizing ethos of hip hop, 24
Dill, Karen, 135–138
Dilulio, John, 76
DJ Star (disc jockey), 106
Dole, Bob, 73
Doug E. Fresh (rap artist), 35
Doyle, Jim, 79
Dr. Dre (rap artist), 108, 121
Drake (rap artist), 33
Drug culture in rap, 95, 125, 130
Duffin, Reilly, 52–53
Dyson, Michael Eric, 106, 132–133

E

Earl (E-40) Stevens (rap artist), 74
Egypt, 16–17, 26, 40, 41
El Général (rap artist), 16, 17, 25–26, 39
El Salvador, 19

Elementz (Cincinnati), 77
Ella Baker Center for Human Rights (Oakland), 77, 78, 80
Emceeing (vocalizing), 22, 32, 52
Eminem (rap artist), 33, 77
EMI records, 99
Emmanuel, Carson, 51
Emmis Communications, 78
European youth culture, 33
Eve (rap artist), 109

F

Fab 5 Freddy (rap artist), 93, 94
Facebook, 17, 25, 40
Faith-Based and Community Initiatives, 76
Fernandez, Sujatha, 39–42
50 Cent (rap artist), 69, 80, 117, 124, 130–131
First Amendment rights, 56, 59
First Nations youth culture, 33
Fisher, Brittany, 54
Foster, Jade, 92–93
France, 34, 141
Fraternal Order of Police, 73
Freedom of speech/expression, 56–57, 137, 138
Fried, Carrie B., 124

G

Gangsta rap
 commercial aspect of, 121
 destructive nature of, 59, 95
 inspiration for, 133
 popularity of, 18, 35, 38, 60
 rejection of, 73, 97, 107
 stereotype of, 16
 street outreach and, 145–146

as violence prevention, 143–146
Garrity, Brian, 97–98
Glass, Brent D., 93
Glocalization concept, 30
Goodwin, Michele, 105–107
Gore, Tipper, 73
Graffiti art and writing, 22, 32, 52, 71, 83, 92
Gramsci, Antonio, 24
Grandmaster Flash (rap artist), 18, 93
Gravenor, J.D., 51–54
Green Job Corps, 78
Green Jobs Act, 78
Gunn, Mark, 43–45

H

Haiti, 19
Hampton, Dream, 116, 117
Harris Publication, 118
Harvard University, 111
Hemmings, Sally, 102
Herrnstein, Richard J., 126
Higgins, Dalton, 32–38
Hill, Lauryn, 90–91
Hip-Hop Archive, 111
Hip-hop culture
 African American influence, 30–31
 antisocial elements of, 95
 breakdancing in, 22, 32, 52, 71, 83, 92
 community of, 24–25
 deejaying in, 22, 71, 83, 92
 emceeing in, 22, 32, 52
 emergence of, 17–18
 graffiti art and writing, 22, 32, 52, 71, 83, 92

hip hop nation, 23–24
importance of, 93–94
as language of the world,
27–28
local and global, 28–29
origins of, 29–30
political impact, 16–20, 26–27,
84–87
rap *vs.*, 22
sound track for revolution,
25–26
success statistics, 27
See also Gangsta rap; Hypersexuality in hip hop; Rap
music; Social justice and hip
hop
Hip-hop culture, global impact
antisocial elements and, 95
commercial success, 32–34
as language of the world,
39–40
multicultural movement,
34–35
overview, 22–23, 32
potential of, 38
profit from, 37–38
raw and uncut nature of, 36–
37, 40–41
sociopolitical change from,
39–42
as unrepentant outlaw music,
35–36
as voice of clarity and leadership, 41–42
of youth, 32–38
Hip-hop culture, influence
campaigning against rap,
59–60
double standards and, 59
on girls, 61–68
greed and, 56–57
growing up with, 53–54

as harmful to African American communities, 55–60
on identity, 52–53
misrepresentation of culture,
58
overview, 51–54, 55–56, 92–93
political empowerment, 81–91
rights and responsibilities, 57
as self-expression for youth,
92–95
social justice concerns, 69–80
success of, 94–95
Hip-hop culture, political empowerment
overview, 81–82
rap and black identity, 83–84
rap can promote, 81–91
relevance of hip hop, 84–87
representation of hip hop,
87–88, 90–91
Hip Hop Diplomacy blog, 17
Hip-hop feminism
black feminism *vs.*, 110–111
as factor in change, 108–113
future of, 111–112
identity of, 112–113
overview, 108–109
rap music and misogyny, 109–
110
Hip-hop nation, 23–24
Hip-Hop Summit Action Network
(HSAN), 76, 79, 98–99
Homicide in lyrics, 125, 130
Homo Hop movement, 34
Horrorcore Rap, 35
House Subcommittee on Commerce, Trade and Consumer
Protection, 132
Hurt, Byron, 75, 118
Hustle & Flow (film), 64–65

Hypersexuality in hip hop
  in film, 64–65
  impact on girls, 61–68
  mixed emotions over, 66–67
  overview, 61–62
  rapping by kids, 65–66
  talking about, 62–64
  women role models and,
    67–68

I

Ibn Thabit (hip-hop artist), 17
Ice Cube (rap artist), 38
Ice-T (rap artist), 37, 73, 93, 97,
  133
Imani, Jakada, 77
Imus, Don comments
  as acceptable, 136
  debate over, 37, 79, 98, 132
  rap influences on, 69–70, 108,
    116–117
  as unacceptable, 59
Incidents in the Life of a Slave Girl
  (Jacob), 103
Inner-city violence, 72–74
Intelligent Hoodlum (rap group),
  73
Interactive Media, 135
International Federation of the
  Phonographic Industry (IFPI),
  22
Interscope Records, 98
Iraq, 69

J

J Dilla (rap artist), 37
Jacob, Harriet, 103
Jay-Z (rap artist), 32–33, 71, 75,
  86–87, 117, 131

Al Jazeera (news source), 25
Jefferson, Thomas, 102
Jena 6 case, 55
Jenkins, Carey, 79
Jim Crow-era racism, 88
Johnson, Bob, 75
Johnson, Lyndon, 59
Jordan, 17

K

Keeping it real ethos, 125–126,
  129
Kerry, John, 85
Keyti (rap artist), 40
Khmer Rouge government, 128
King, Stephen, 129
Kitwana, Baraki, 110
Klezmer Rap, 35
Klunk, Paige, 19
Koehler-Derrick, Beatrice, 61–68
Kool G. Rap (rap group), 73
Kool Herc (rap artist), 93
KRS-ONE (rap artist), 72
Kump, Anessa, 54
Kuwait, 17
Kweli, Talbi, 88

L

Latin American youth culture, 22,
  33, 94
Law and Order (TV show), 123
League of Young Voters, 71, 77
Lear, Norman, 90
Led Zeppelin (rock group), 71
Lee, Nicole, 80, 144–145
Leyden, Peter, 77
Libya, 17, 26, 40
Lieberman, Joe, 73

Lil' John (rap artist), 124
Lil' Kim (rap artist), 112
Lil' Wayne (rap artist), 108
Limbaugh, Rush, 101
Literary art of rap music, 46–49
Lo, Papa Moussa, 41
Los Angeles Police Department
  (LAPD), 37
Lovebug Starski (rap artist), 32
Lucas, George, 83
Ludacris (rap artist), 124, 128
Lynette, Nicki, 112

M

Malcolm X Grassroots Movement
  (Brooklyn), 77
Al-Masry Al-Youm (newspaper),
  26
Master Mimz (hip hop artist), 26
Master P. (rap artist), 133
Mbalax music, 40
MC Lyte (rap artist), 93, 109
McCain, John, 82
McGill University, 51
Media violence, 135–136
Meters (rock group), 71
Middle East, 16, 25, 81, 122
Middle Eastern youth culture, 26,
  33
Miller, Percy, 133
Milloy, Courtland, 59
Minaj, Nicki, 111–112
Misogyny and hip-hop culture,
  61–68
Missouri Press Association, 103
Morgan, Andy, 16
Morgan, Joan, 108, 109–110, 111,
  117

Morgan, Marcyliena, 22–31, 111,
  113
Morocco, 17
Morris, Doug, 134
Moseley-Braun, Carol, 73
Motown music, 94
Moynihan, Daniel Patrick, 104
Mubarak, Hosni, 16, 26
Multicultural movement, 34–35
Murphy, Eddie, 101
Murray, Charles, 126

N

Nas (hip hop artist), 18, 79, 89–90
National Association for the Ad-
  vancement of Colored People
  (NAACP), 98, 106
National Congress of Black
  Women, 60
National Council for Black Stud-
  ies, 19
National Hip-Hop Political Con-
  vention, 71, 76–77
National Museum of American
  History, 92
National Political Congress of
  Black Women, 99
National Rifle Association, 73
Native American youth culture,
  35, 56–57
N'Dour, Youssou, 40, 42
Neal, Mark Anthony, 113, 117–118
Nelly (rap artist), 108, 117
Nerdcore Rap, 34
New York Times (newspaper), 122–
  123
Ngoka, Noel, 53
Nigeria, 33

North Africa, 25

N.W.A. (Niggaz With Attitude), 37, 44, 73, 120

N-word ban, 79, 98

O

Oakland City Council, 117

Obama, Barack election
    as black president, 88–90
    campaign of, 82–86
    overview, 43, 81–82
    representation of hip hop, 87–88

Occupying Hip Hop, 45

100 Black Men and Safe Passages, 114

O'Reilly, Bill, 70, 128

Orfori-Atta, Akoto, 108–113

OutKast (rap group), 94

P

P. Diddy. See Sean (P. Diddy) Combs

Paris (rap group), 73

Pate, Alexs, 46–49

Pelosi, Nancy, 78

Percy (Master P) Miller (rap artist), 74

Perez, Marvette, 92, 93, 95

Perry, Imani, 30–31

Philthy Rich (rap artist), 143–146

Polanco-Simmons, Shaun, 52

Political impact of hip hop, 16–20

Porter, Paul, 74–75, 79

Presley, Elvis, 33

Protest rap, 25

Public Enemy (rap group), 18, 33, 44, 71–72, 120

Puerto Rican youth culture, 90

Q

Queen Latifah (actor, singer), 73, 108, 109

Quickley, Jerry, 69–71

R

Racism
    black culture and, 106
    in hip hop, 27, 38, 43, 120, 127
    impact of, 137
    n-word usage, 37
    in rap music, 73, 133, 136
    subconscious racism, 141

Rap music
    accountability of artists, 45
    as apathetic, 43–45
    black identity and, 83–84
    campaigning against, 59–60
    drug culture in, 95, 125, 130
    emceeing, 32
    hip hop vs., 22
    as literary art form, 46–49
    monoculture of, 74–75
    origins, 29–30
    overview, 43–44, 46–47
    protest rap, 25
    reading rap/poetry, 47–48
    self-reflection in, 48–49
    social justice and, 69–80
    thug rap, 75–79
    See also Gangsta rap

Rap music, and misogyny
    b-word (bitch) usage, 37, 52, 54, 59, 64, 104

defense against black women, 103

degrading rap videos, 105–107

hip-hop community addresses, 114–118

hip-hop feminism, 108–113

objectifies, degrades and exploits, 101–104

overview, 101

roots of disrespect, 102–103

scrutiny of lyrics, 97–98

self-scrutiny and, 103–104, 116–117

Rap music, and violence

assumptions about, 141

behavioral problems and academic achievement, 140–141

causality and, 121–123

context consideration in, 130–131

debate over, 120–131

interpretation of lyrics, 124–127

listener affected by, 135–138

listener not affected by, 139–142

mass media and, 136

middle ground stance over, 129–130

music industry exploitation of, 132–134

overview, 120–121, 132–133, 135–136, 139–140

popular media and, 123–124

protection of society from, 127–129

regulation needed, 137–139

Rap videos as degrading, 105–107

Rapping by kids, 65–66, 92

R.E.A.C.Hip-Hop (New York City), 78

Recording Industry Association of America (RIAA), 27, 94

Rock the Vote, 76

Rose, Tricia, 120–131

Rosen, Hilary, 99–100

Rosenthal, Andrew, 122

Rove, Karl, 77

Run-D.M.C. (rap artist), 94

Rush, Bobby, 79–80, 132

Russia, 19

S

Satten, Vanessa, 118

Schwarzenegger, Arnold, 123

Sean (P. Diddy) Combs (rap artist), 71, 76, 83, 90

Self-reflection in rap music, 48–49

Selling My Brothers (Ashhurst), 74

Senegal, 19

Sharpley-Whiting, Tracy, 101–104

Sharpton, Al, 98

Shawn (Jay-Z) Carter (rap artist), 74

Shimmel, Mark, 93–95

Simmons, Olis, 145

Simmons, Russell, 70–74, 76, 79, 93, 98

Slumlording, 72

Smith, Will, 73

Smithsonian Institution, 92

Snoop Dogg (rap artist), 38, 97, 117, 121

Social justice and hip hop

origins of, 72–74

overview, 69–71

rap exposure and, 69–80

rap monoculture, 74–75

thug rap, 75–79

Solis, Hilda, 78

Sound track for revolution, 25–26
South Asian youth culture, 33
Southwest Youth Collaborative/
  University of Hip-Hop
  (Chicago), 77
Space Cowboy (rap artist), 32
Spain, 19
Sparks, Kyle, 54
Spelman College, 117
Spence, Lester, 81–86
Spielberg, Steven, 83
Steffans, Karrine, 104
Sting (pop singer), 83
Stoute, Steve, 18–19
Street culture, 130
Subconscious racism, 141
Sugarhill Gang (rap group), 70
Suicidal ideation, 141
Syria, 17

T

Talking-over technique, 92
*The Tanning of America: How Hip-
  Hop Created a Culture That Re-
  wrote the Rules of the New
  Economy* (Stoute), 18–19
Tarantino, Quentin, 101
Tea Party, 44
Teixeira, Ruy, 77
Thiat (rap artist), 39, 41
Thomas, Isiah, 59
Thug rap, 75–79
T.I. (rap artist), 124
Time (magazine), 25
Time Warner, 98, 99
Tone, Tony, 72
Too Short (rap artist), 114–118,
  145

Torian, Troi, 106
Touré, Cheikh Oumar Cyrille, 39
Translocal hip hop, 29
Trudell, John, 34
Tucker, C. Delores, 58, 73, 99
Tunisia, 17, 25, 26, 40
Tupac (2Pac) Shakur (hip hop
  artist), 25, 97, 109, 117, 130
Turntabalism, 22
21st Century Youth Leadership
  Project (Selma), 77
24 (TV show), 123
Twitter, 17
2 Live Crew (rap group), 117

U

Underground hip hop, 28–29
United Kingdom (UK), 38
Universal Music, 134
University of Chicago, 70, 76
Urban fashion, 52
Urban Peace Movement, 144
USA Today (newspaper), 17

V

Viacom, 134
Video game violence, 121–122,
  135–137
Violence-prevention efforts, 143
*A Voice from the South, by A
  Woman from the South* (Cooper),
  103

W

Wade, Abdoulaye, 41–42
Walker, Carolee, 92–95
Walter, Shoshana, 143–146

Warner Music Group (WMG), 79,
 97, 99
Washington Post (newspaper), 59
Waterflow (rap artist), 41
Watson, Jim, 126
We Are the 44
Coalition, 116, 117–118
W.E.B. Du Bois Institute, 111
Wells, Ida B., 103
West, Kanye, 77, 80, 88, 111
*When Chickenheads Come Home
 to Roost: My Life as a Hip-Hop
 Feminist* (Morgan), 109
Williams, E. Faye, 55–60
Winfrey, Oprah, 70
Wiz Kalifah (rap artist), 45
Wolof language, 41
Women role models, 67–68

Women's Coalition for Dignity
 and Diversity, 59

X

XXL Magazine, 117, 118

Y

Yemen, 17
Y'en a Marre movement, 42
Yo! MTV Raps (TV show), 18
Young Jeezy (rap artist), 36
Youth Media Council (Oakland),
 78
Youth Organizing Project
 (Boston), 77
Youth Uprising, 145–146
YouTube, 17, 25, 40